THE SHOOTING *a Memoir*

Kemp Powers

THUNDER'S MOUTH PRESS • NEW YORK

THE SHOOTING: A MEMOIR

Published by
Thunder's Mouth Press
An Imprint of Avalon Publishing Group Inc.
245 West 17th St., 11th Floor
New York, NY 10011

AVALON
publishing group incorporated

Library of Congress Cataloging-in-Publication Data is available.

ISBN 1-56858-320-6

9 8 7 6 5 4 3 2 1

Book design by Maria Elias
Printed in the United States of America
Distributed by Publishers Group West

In loving memory of R.O.

How I came to this

I don't know if we can ever truly atone for our sins. I once thought it was absolutely the case. God knows I've spent enough years trying to do so. My friend Henry's death silently hung over me for much of my childhood, but I'd finally begun to heed my mother's advice to "let sleeping dogs lie." Then came the night of March 15, 2000.

We were living in Queens: my then wife, my two-year-old daughter, and I. It was quite a haul for my wife and me from Highland Avenue in Jamaica to our jobs, mine in Chelsea, hers in Harlem, but it was worth it if it meant living in a neighborhood that was peaceful and quiet. Emotionally, things were anything but. Henry's death had come roaring back into the forefront of my thoughts thanks to my daughter's near death from a bout with febrile seizures. My child's mortality was a constant concern, but despite these and other distressing matters, I kept my inner anxieties a secret even from those who were closest to me. Unfortunately, it had become common practice for me to withdraw and become more solitary when I felt emotionally overwhelmed.

That was, until Patrick Dorismond's unlikely death at the hand of New York's finest. If you lived anywhere other than

New York City in 2000, you've probably never heard of Patrick Dorismond, but in the then shaky tenure of Mayor Rudolph Giuliani, Dorismond became an exclamation point in a long chain of police brutality cases that began with Abner Louima in 1997.

Unlike Louima, the well-known Haitian immigrant who was sodomized with a plunger by several police officers and became a national name thanks to the involvement of flamboyant personalities such as Al Sharpton, the Dorismond case was much lower profile. But for me, the Patrick Dorismond incident was the single most important case of political misconduct in the city's history. His experience caused me to think for long hours about atonement, and is the primary reason I decided to tell my story.

Pre-September 11 New York was a time when Giuliani's zero-tolerance policies toward crime had made the city the safest it'd been in decades—but simultaneously put the mayor and the police force at odds with almost all of New York's minority ethnic communities. Claims of civil rights violations ran rampant, and it seemed as though every week the mayor had to hold a press conference to explain away some new misdeed.

Patrick Dorismond was the twenty-six-year-old father of two young children, and he had aspirations of becoming a police officer. At the time, he was working as a security guard in Manhattan. Dorismond and a friend stopped the night of March 15 at a bar for a beer after work, and were approached by an undercover police officer posing as a drug dealer. It was part of an elaborate sting operation called "Operation Condor" that was rooting out potential narcotics customers, and had already netted more than eighteen thousand arrests in only two months.

The operation's premise is simple. The undercover officer simply approaches a person in one of the designated areas and attempts to sell him drugs. When the person agrees and tries to make the purchase, he's arrested on the spot. However, things did not go according to plan when the undercover officer approached Dorismond. Rather than agree to the deal or just ignore the dealer, Dorismond became enraged, and here the testimonials differ. According to police, Dorismond struck the officer. Several witnesses at the scene claimed that the undercover cop was the aggressor. Nonetheless, when the smoke cleared, Patrick Dorismond lay dead, shot by the police for doing something any suburban parent would be saluted for: confronting a drug dealer.

Of course this was a terrible public relations blunder for an already embattled mayor. Police had only recently been acquitted for unleashing a fusillade on unarmed immigrant Amadou Diallo when they mistook his wallet for a weapon, and this was yet another sign that the policies of the department and the mayor himself were too cavalier in distinguishing between black criminals and black citizens. Dorismond was not a career criminal. His record was clean. In fact, it was so clean that the administration had to dig into his juvenile record to find any transgressions whatsoever. As it turns out, Dorismond had been arrested for robbery in 1987, when he was only thirteen years old. The mayor claimed in front of a press assemblage that Dorismond "was no altar boy"—insinuating, without saying it, that Dorismond had his fate coming.

This guy was no altar boy. The interesting irony that

Dorismond was indeed an altar boy as a child was overshadowed by the fact that his charge of assault as a teenager made him a career criminal in the eyes of many. It didn't matter that this happened during his teenage years, that the arrest reportedly came as the result of a fistfight over a quarter, or that the record of his transgression was supposed to have been sealed and then expunged when he turned sixteen. It didn't even matter that his death came as he was trying to do the right thing —the exact thing many a public service announcement has urged us to do. When Patrick Dorismond was gone, he became another dead nigger with a record.

It was disheartening. It was enraging. If this man was no altar boy, then I was the anti-Christ. Hadn't I done enough good to deserve not to have my entire life encapsulated by that single event? I hadn't touched a gun since that afternoon back in 1988. I'd never touched an illegal drug. I didn't even drink (back then). I did everything I could at every turn to help others. Did any of it matter?

The short answer was, at least in some eyes, no. And the sobering dose of that reality depressed me. I could one day unwittingly find myself on the receiving end of some misunderstood person's knife, bullet, or worse. If that happened, would the people having those postmortem conversations describe me only as a juvenile felon? Given, what I did was absolutely indefensible. But at least I'm going to have a voice in the single event that may one day come to encapsulate my life. At least I'm going to have a voice if people decide to hold a discussion about the Shooting.

Part One.

When I was fourteen, I shot my best friend in the face and watched him die. I'm not trying to sound cold when I say it like that. I'm not a criminal, at least not to the people who matter. Not to my family. Not to his family. Not to my friends. Not even to the state of New York. Still, just typing these words shocks me; I see them taking shape across the screen and I can't believe the actions I'm describing are my own. In the fifteen years since it happened, I haven't discussed the incident in detail with a single person.

Henry was one of seven homicides that day in New York City. At fourteen, he wasn't even the youngest—a twelve-year-old from Queens held that distinction. But his was the death I saw with my own eyes, the one I caused with my own hand, the one I will carry for the rest of my life.

Henry and I met through a mutual friend in seventh grade, and we got along from the start. We both stood out from the crowd. He was unusually broad and muscular for a twelve-year-old, and I was so tall and skinny that every school gym session brought on a round of jeering comparisons to Manute Bol, that seven-foot, seven-inch twig of a basketball player from the Sudan. Henry and I were as physically different as two teenagers could be.

Within just a few months of that first junior high school year we were close friends. We walked together to the subway station every day after school, we read comic books and we shared a hatred for the bullies from nearby John Jay High School, who'd tease us and show up on Halloween to rain rotten eggs, batteries, and water balloons on us. We talked about things in a way our other friends couldn't understand. We were best friends.

Home was a tidy two-bedroom co-op on the second floor of a small brick building in the Kensington section of Brooklyn, a typical border neighborhood populated by Hasidim, Eastern Europeans, blacks, and Puerto Ricans. Our small apartment was a source of pride for my mother, who'd raised my three older sisters and me single-handedly since splitting with my father when I was four. I occasionally saw and heard from Dad, but he was mostly a stranger in my life.

Mom worked full-time as a nurse at an old-folks home fifteen blocks from our apartment and was also a captain in the Army Reserve. She kept four guns in the apartment. Her military background, combined with an interest in firearms, had turned her into something of a collector. One of her guns was an antique flintlock pistol. I called it the cowboy gun because it reminded me of the huge, heavy revolvers Clint Eastwood wielded with such cool authority in those old spaghetti westerns. The cowboy gun was strictly a collector's item. She also kept a .22 caliber semiautomatic rifle (with a scope), a .25 caliber semiautomatic pistol, and a .38 caliber snub-nosed revolver.

When I turned twelve, Mom took me on my first trip to the range, where I had a chance to try out all the guns. The .22 rifle, with its glossy wood stock and endless barrel, had always struck me as being pretty. At the range, I found that it was easy to use and very accurate, thanks to the scope. But the low caliber made me feel like I was firing a BB gun.

The .25 pistol was my favorite. I loved that it was small and silver and looked almost like a toy, with a loop of dingy white masking tape wrapped around the handle. I loved the tiny five-shot clip. I also loved that it had less kick than the .38, which made it a good range gun, easy to fire with accuracy.

The .38 was the intimidator. The fact that it was a revolver played right into all my fantasies. Anyone who'd seen *Taxi Driver* knew what a snub-nosed .38 looked like and what its reputation was. "The .38, that's a fine gun," the dealer told Robert De Niro as De Niro aimed and pointed it out the window. "You could hammer nails with that gun all day, come back, and it would still cut dead center on target every time." The one in the movie was silver with a pearl grip. Mom's was service-style, black metal with a brown wooden grip. It felt much heavier in my hand than the .25—which I took as a sign of its power. It felt dense. It kicked hard when I fired it. Mom kept it just inside her armoire near a box filled with bullets. It was the gun she kept handy for personal protection.

When Mom wasn't around, I taught myself to spin the .38 on the tip of my index finger like an Old West quick-draw artist. I showed off all three guns to my friends and even let them handle them. They'd come by after school, in the hours before Mom got home from work, and we'd play with the guns.

By freshman year in high school, Henry was a regular visitor. We'd started going to different schools, but he'd hop the F train right after classes let out, and he'd be waiting for me in front of my building by the time I got off the bus.

On the afternoon of April 14, 1988, Mom called from the nursing home where she worked to say I wasn't allowed to have any friends over that day. "I just want to come home and get some rest," she said, explaining she was exhausted from all the work she'd been doing lately. "Okay," I said, and hung up the phone, failing to mention that Henry and another friend, Chris, were already on their way over. Not to worry, though: Mom wouldn't get home until 5:30 or so, which would give us plenty of time to hang out. They'd be gone before she even set foot in the apartment.

When Henry and Chris arrived, we went straight to my bedroom. Henry dropped his backpack and coat onto the floor and plopped down on my bed. Our apartment was a one-bedroom unit when Mom bought it, but in an effort to give me some privacy (my three older sisters having moved out), she had erected a wall with a door in the living room to create a second bedroom for me. To compensate for the wall's blocking out sunlight to the now smaller living room, my bedroom walls weren't built all the way up to the ceiling, instead yielding about twelve inches of space, enough to let a sliver of light through. I loved that room. I kept the walls white, free of posters—I'd moved around enough to know that removing a favorite poster from a wall would only result in its destruction. I used a couple of large pillows to dress my bed up like a sofa so friends would have a place to sit and hang out. It made my room feel like my own little apartment.

I can't recall how the .38 came out. I was probably just showing off Mom's gun again. By this time, I'd been to the range several times and had mastered my index-finger spin, so I fancied myself somewhat of an expert. I'd even devised a game where I would insert a bullet into one of the chambers, spin the cylinder and then lock it into place for a game of Russian roulette. In reality, I'd either palm the bullet and discreetly drop it onto the floor, or place it a few notches away from the chamber so there was no bullet in the barrel when the trigger was pulled. I can't even count how many times I pointed it at my head, at walls, at friends, and pulled the trigger to their shock and subsequent amusement. It was something I thought I was good at. It made me feel tough.

Anyway, with Henry and Chris sitting on my bed, I started my routine. First I demonstrated the index finger spin. Then I pretended to insert a bullet randomly, spun the cylinder, and pointed the gun at Henry. I smiled and pulled the trigger, ready to shout "Gotcha!" after making him flinch. Only instead of the dull click of the hammer followed by laughter, there was a deafening explosion and a flash of light. The smell of gunpowder filled my room. Chris and Henry turned away, their backs to me, and my initial thought was that I must have just fired into the wall. The silence was complete. In the endless second after the gun went off, it was as though everything was moving in slow motion.

● ● ●

2003.

It seemed like the only thing anyone ever caught on the pier was crabs. And not just the old guys dropping crab cages into the murky water. Everyone with a rod and reel caught them. You'd drop your pole over the edge, get a bite, and start reeling in your prize, anxious that a bluefish or a flounder would be flapping on the end of your line. When the end of the line and the hook finally emerged from the water, it was always a crab dangling by one arm. And it always let go just a split second before you got it to the pier, flipping a crustacean "fuck you" with its claw as it splashed back into the water and scuttled off to take someone else's bait.

Oh, there were guys on the pier with fish. By the time my dad and I arrived, they already had buckets full of them. From bluefish to the pan-frying variety. But I never saw anyone pull these magnificent scaled beasts from the darkness of the water, and after a while I started to suspect the guys had brought them from an aquarium and were just holding them in the bucket for show—like they were on consignment from the city of New York to lure more suckers to the Coney Island pier and waste what little money they had on nightcrawlers.

Considering how we were never fruitful, it made no sense why I enjoyed going to the pier so much with Dad. Maybe it was because it was the only father-son activity we participated in. Maybe it was because I secretly believed we'd catch that bluefish he always said we would. Back then, none of the grime and decay of Coney Island, or Brooklyn in general, ever seemed as bad or as sad as it would in hindsight years later. And it was always better than dropping our lines over on the

Belt Parkway, watching oil tankers and cargo ships slowly float past, as traffic from the Verrazano-Narrows Bridge rumbled overhead. At least we were facing the great green and brown expanse of the Atlantic Ocean, and thousands of miles away I knew some kid was sitting on a pier in Portugal with his dad, having the bait snatched off of his line by some fucking crab.

I don't recall exactly how old I was, but I can remember a number of my life's firsts out there in Coney Island. I can remember my first slice of pizza. I was a finicky eater, even for a young child. I loved hamburgers and loved cheese, but refused to eat cheeseburgers because the texture of melted cheese made my stomach turn. When it came to pizza, either of the isosceles triangle or square Sicilian variety, I thought the melted cheese and tomato sauce combination was downright horrific. My three older sisters one day took me to a parlor on the corner. They cajoled me to at least *try* a slice. After finally conceding and taking a bite, I chased them home, begging for pizza all the way.

I can remember my first time wading into the waters in Coney Island. I was finally big enough that I'd overcome my fear of being washed away by the tide and could join the teeming throng that populated the beach during the summer months. I took those first steps into the water, and before I knew it, I was waist-deep, smiling with a sudden burst of confidence uncalled for by a child who couldn't even swim. I dropped to my knees so my head was completely submerged. I'd practiced in city pools several times for this moment. I just knew when I opened my eyes I'd be greeted by an amazing undersea medley, with colorful fish dancing between the legs of the swimmers. I opened my eyes to the searing pain and murky darkness of countless pollutants mixed with salt and sand. I exploded from the water like I was drowning, rubbing my red eyes and trying desperately to orient myself. When my eyes finally cleared, I saw a man standing about five feet in front of me, the water up to his knees. His shorts were down around his thighs and he was taking a piss.

Oh, God, it's good to be back in Brooklyn! These are the thoughts that usually come to mind on my frequent return trips to the borough that raised and nurtured me. It's tough for the casual observer to know what the big deal is about Brooklyn, and trying to explain it is akin to trying to explain quantum physics to a toddler. Brooklyn is those tiny experiences, unique to each homegrown son and daughter, yet so shared that it makes us part of this great dysfunctional family.

I'm walking with Mike, one of my closest friends since we were both a foot shorter, talking about how much the city has changed. He asks me what changes I've noticed the most, and I respond without hesitation.

"Blondes."

He looks puzzled.

"Come on man. When we were kids, the only white people in Brooklyn were Italians, Jews, and Eastern Europeans. Blondes were something we only saw on television, and now they're everywhere. They even fucking show up in Fort Greene."

Mike gets it, then laughs out loud. He's never left Brooklyn, and is always entertained by my musings when I return home. I left New York with my mother in 1989. I'd returned to live in the city postcollege, my pregnant wife in tow, but I returned to

Queens, not the Brooklyn neighborhood where I grew up—
thanks mainly to the borough's sudden popularity among
artistic types and Manhattan expatriates who loved to exclaim
"can you believe I live in Brooklyn?" to their friends over
dinner as a sign of *nouveau cool*.

I've flown into New York for the weekend from my home in
Chicago, and Mike and I are taking a stroll, literally, down
memory lane. Usually, when I make my jaunts back into town for
business or pleasure, I either stay in a hotel in Union Square
(business) or with my aunt Minnie out in the familiar climes of
Coney Island (pleasure). When my old friends and I do hang
out, it's in Manhattan. But today I'm on Mike's block in Kensington, not far from where I lived when the two of us attended
high school together.

Passing through this part of Brooklyn is a rarity—as should
be expected when neighborhood highlights include a cemetery
and a Burger King. Mike's dad dug graves at that cemetery.
Buzz-A-Rama, the slot-car racing arcade at Church Avenue
and Dahill Road, was as big a part of our childhood as the
cemetery or Space Harrier or Arlene's gigantic tits. Five enormous, colored tracks took up most of the floor space, and
arcade games dotted the empty spaces not occupied by tracks.
A group of us could rent any of the tracks in the place for an
hour at a time. Any except the infamous blue track, which was
the largest in the arcade and was reserved for those with their
own cars (we rented ours from the shop). We'd simply pay our
few dollars, select a beat-up model stock car, then connect the
small jumper cables of the trigger to one of eight lanes, and
we'd race away the afternoon.

Venturing into the place now is like walking through a time

warp. The original owner, Buzzy, still oversees the place from his perch at the front desk, all haggard and gray from years of watching over mischievous children. More shockingly, the same old arcade games are still operating, including the Gauntlet II game we'd pump endless quarters into after school. Buzzy says he's kept the old coin-op games functional so that younger children can have something to do when the place hosts birthday parties.

I mention how I haven't been here in more than a decade, hoping to start a nostalgic conversation with the owner. Instead, Buzzy bitterly recounts how some of the machines were busted beyond repair during various robberies over the years.

"One time, after robbin' the place, do you know what they did?" he says. "They took a shit on the floor, right over there."

Mike and I decide that we can't visit the place after all these years and not race for a while. So, Mike, my other friend Ornette, and I slap down a few dollars and get to racing on the orange track. Almost as soon as our cars take off from the starting point, they jump the track and slam into the walls. One by one, each of us runs over to set his car back, while the other two continue trying to race, only to have their cars inevitably jump the track just a few seconds later. Within five minutes, we're all doubling over in laughter at the monotony of the experience, and wondering why it held such an allure when we were kids.

Along with "The Dungeon," a small basement deli across the street from our junior high school that was renown for its one-dollar hero sandwiches, Buzzy's was an icon. Despite the place's weathered appearance, there was a comfort to be found in its continued existence.

"And some of the best games are still working," Mike says, pointing out the old Zaxxon console that ate an endless number of our quarters.

Henry never came to Buzzy's though.

"What?" Mike asks, somewhat shocked.

Henry never came here after school. It was too far away from where he lived.

"You still think about him?"

Yes.

"A lot?"

Every day.

Mike is stunned, and isn't sure what to say. He pauses for several seconds before finally giving me a response.

"Fuuuuuuuck. How many years ago was that? When Henry . . . died?"

Fifteen years. It was 1988.

• • •

My ears were hot, ringing; my heart began to pound. Chris turned around, and we both looked at Henry, his back still to us, and waited for him to turn around, to say he was okay, to laugh and tell me how much trouble I'd be in when my mom got home.

I couldn't figure out how a bullet had gotten into the chamber.

Henry turned to face us, covering his mouth, and he lowered his hands. There was a hole the size of a nickel in his chin, just below his lips. He looked at me and opened his mouth.

"Gnnnaaaaaaaaaaaaaaaaa!"

He looked like he wanted to scream in pain but couldn't because something was lodged in his throat. Then he opened his mouth and vomited more blood than I'd ever seen in my life, and it poured thickly into his lap and onto my burgundy comforter. We locked terrified eyes.

My first thought was *cover the wound.* Mom was a nurse, and she always taught me to cover a bleeding wound. So I ran out of the room to the linen closet and grabbed a towel, almost slipping on the hardwood floor as I sped through the doorway. By the time I made it back, Henry had staggered into the living room. He was catching the blood pouring from his wound in his trembling hands, and it was spilling over onto the floor. His eyes were wide with shock. I placed the towel over his chin and ran to the phone.

I dialed as fast as I could. "Mom, get home quick! Henry's been shot!" I screamed, and hung up as Henry fell forward onto his face. A large pool of blood spread across the floor. He began to convulse. His head shook back and forth, a horrible gurgling sound building up in his throat. I ran to him and screamed at Chris to call the police. I tried to flip Henry over but couldn't. He was too heavy, too big. I was too weak. The blood kept pouring out.

"What's the address?" screamed Chris.

I blurted out my address, then stood and bounced around and around in circles like a manic animal. Chris flipped Henry over. Henry's eyes were closed. I told Chris I'd get help, and I ran for the door. I could hear Chris sobbing in the background as he cradled Henry's head and spoke to him.

"I love you Henry," he said. "I love you. I love you."

I began hammering on my neighbors' doors, begging for help. How could it be that no one was home in the entire building? Finally, a man came to the door at the end of the hall. "Please come help me!" I screamed, relieved that I'd found an adult who could help. "My friend's been shot! Please help!"

He looked down the hall at my open door, then looked back at me, at my Miami Dolphins sweatshirt stained with blood.

"I'm sorry," he said. "I can't help you."

Then he closed his door.

Total panic now, and I was running in circles again, trying to think. What could I do? Who could I call? What the fuck had I done? Was this real? Why was this happening?

A thought popped into my head: *there are people on the street who can help!* Down the staircase I went. As I burst into the lobby, two police officers walked in—the first respondents to Chris's call. I grabbed one by the arm, repeating my frantic plea. "Please help me! My friend's been shot! Please help! Please!" I must have been stammering terribly because the officers both looked confused as I led them up the stairs to my apartment. I remember feeling a sense of relief as I approached the door because I knew the police would be able to save him. They would make things right. I pointed to Henry, lying on the floor beside my bedroom in a pool of blood.

"There he is! Please help him! Help him!"

I expected them to spring into action, doing that thing they do on television, pulling Henry back from the brink of death with their miraculous paramedic skills. Instead, one officer stepped warily into my apartment and called for help on his radio. The other tried to calm me down, but by now I was jumping up and down, screaming the same words over and over as tears ran down my cheeks, thinking the words could somehow save Henry.

"Help him! Help him! Help him! Help him! Help him!"

The next thing I knew, the hallway was full of people. Mom was there, sobbing. The paramedics were there. More police officers were there. The neighbor who wouldn't help us earlier was there, smiling and chatting with the cops. Chris and I were there, standing in the hall, when a paramedic came out of my apartment.

"How is he?" I asked. "How is he? Is he going to be okay?"

I don't know what I expected his response to be, but I wasn't prepared for his words.

"He's gone."

I'd never seen the inside of a police station before, but it felt familiar. It had the same worn, institutional look as my junior high school. I ended up in what looked like a conference room, running through the details with the cops, as my mom, dad, and a few aunts and uncles looked on in shock. I wanted to crawl under the table and go to sleep. Maybe then I could stop shaking.

The police took me to a room and handed me a placard, which I held while they snapped several mug shots. As I was being processed, an officer walked in and showed some Polaroids to the guy taking my fingerprints. The photos were taken at what would later be called the "crime scene." I caught a glimpse of one. It was of Henry. He was on his back, mouth open, blood covering his face. There was no chance the paramedics could have been mistaken. Henry was not in a hospital bed, wounded but alive. He was gone.

Henry's family decided not to press charges. Beyond all reason, they embraced me at his wake and offered their forgiveness. They were an older Puerto Rican couple, and there was a look of tired compassion in their faces that one would expect from grieving parents trying their best to forgive. The mother forced out a weak smile, barely making eye contact before looking over to the father for some kind of guidance. The father had none, offering only a similar smile and shrug as he searched for what to say. They spoke very little English, so they gestured to their other son, James, and asked him to tell me they forgave me. Then came the hugs. James shook my hand. "As far as I'm concerned," he said, "I've got a new brother." It felt like he meant it.

Later, when the Brooklyn district attorney hit me with a long list of charges (various degrees of manslaughter and assault, among them), Henry's parents were the ones who spoke about not wanting to destroy two young lives instead of one. I thanked them outside the courtroom that day, fifteen years ago, after the judge decided my punishment would be a year's worth of counseling sessions. The judge seemed disappointed in their plea for compassion, and I could feel his contempt as he had me recount the story of the accident in detail, the last time I'd talk about it until now. Then he gestured to Henry's family and asked them if they were satisfied. They said yes. Even now it seems like an impossible act of charity: the ultimate gift, given to a person who didn't deserve one.

● ● ●

2001.

I'm back in Brooklyn for the day. It's the fifty-third wedding anniversary of my great-uncle, and the event has turned into an impromptu family reunion. I'm meeting people for the first time who say they've known me my entire life. While my daughter chases after her little cousins, Mom ushers me over to meet a cousin I haven't seen in years. I don't remember him at all, and he seems to be having trouble remembering me, too. Then his eyes light up.

"Oh, yeah!" he says. "I remember you! You had that drama with the gun when you were little."

I look around to see if anyone else heard him. *Did he just say what I think he said?* I don't remember what he said after that. I couldn't hear anything, my heart was beating so loud. I excused myself and headed to the buffet.

Someone actually brought it up.

In the years since my appearance in court, no one—not my mother, not my father, not my sisters, not my friends—had ever uttered a single word about the Shooting or about Henry. The people around me seemed to go on with their lives as though Henry had never existed. The incident was officially wiped from my record by the time I was sixteen, and if I never mentioned it again, it would never come up.

That it was out of other people's minds couldn't stop me from thinking about it.

In fact, it was years before I could stop thinking about the Shooting, and Henry, every day. As an adult, whenever some horrendous crime involving a teenager made the news, I'd shudder as friends or colleagues went on about the need to be unmerciful, to punish these animals, regardless of circumstances. I'd awake in the middle of the night and stare at the ceiling, obsessing over my mistake, over Henry's death. I couldn't decide whether the facts that it was an accident, that I was a kid, that I was so sorry, were good enough for me to be absolved.

A month after the reunion, I decide to call my mom to talk to her about that day. I want to find out if her silence all these years has been because she's really forgotten about it and moved on, or whether she's been hiding her feelings, too.

She answers the phone, and I start the conversation by saying how much fun I had at the party in Brooklyn. Then I ask her. Out of the blue. *How did that day affect you?*

There is a long pause.

"You'd think this is something you wouldn't want to talk about," she says. "Something like this, you'd want to try to put it behind you."

But I've been trying to put it behind me. I can't make it go away.

"How do you think *I* feel? I was all alone. I was hurting for you. I was hurting for Henry's family. You were fourteen. You were just a kid."

Were you angry at me?

"I was blaming myself. I should have had that gun locked up, but I didn't. I just never thought you'd mess with it."

Her responses get shorter, more agitated, with every question, and I can hear her breathing during the long periods of silence.

"I don't know how I avoided a nervous breakdown," she says. "A part of me died that day, too, and I know I lost a part of you. Why would you want to talk about this?"

Because I'm going to write about it.

"*Why?*"

Because this is my story.

"I'm going to get off the phone now. I don't like talking about this. It upsets me."

Half my lifetime isn't long enough to wait for us to talk about this?

Silence.

I know you're upset, but how upset do you think I am? I'm the one who did it.

Silence.

I can't just erase it from my memory and pretend it never happened, and I'm never going to get over it and I'm never going to forget about it and move on, because it's a part of my life now, just like it's a part of yours. I'm just trying to learn to live with it. . . .

I finally stop after realizing that I'm not saying any of these things out loud. I stopped speaking after she said I was upsetting her, and I'm thinking this tirade in my head. Mom is still there, silent, on the other end of the line, waiting to be released.

Stranahan, JHS 142, Brooklyn, NY
GRADUATION AUTOGRAPH BOOK
1987

Kemper:
I hope to see you in the tenth grade. Too bad I gotta go to that shit school. Until we meet again . . . good shooting!
—A.L.

Kemp:
Good luck in your new school and kick some white boy's ass!
—Anthony G.

Hey Kempy-Hempy:
I like the color blue, I like the color black
But when it comes to you and guns, you're a wack!

—*Johnny*

Dear Kemp:
It would have been nice to see you more often. I really think you've got a lot going for you! Best of luck in high school. I know you can succeed if you want to.

—*Mrs. Greenfield*

Dear Kemp:
Good luck in Murrow. I know you'll be a huge success. I'll be willing to bet on it.

—*Love, Suzanne*

Kemp:
You've been good to me all the years I've known you. Good luck and may the force be with you.

—*Eddie*

To my good friend Kemp . . . Nigger:
God made you. He made you at night. God was in such a hurry, he forgot to make you white.
PB4Ugo2Bed

—*Your white friend,*
Mikey

Dear Kemp:
Good luck in Murrow and in whichever one of the armed forces you decide to join. I hope you get into West Point and smoke

some pot and grow your afro real long and march for peace on the lawn of the white house with your machine gun in your army personnel mover. Stay Groovy.

—*Samantha*

P.S. Try to keep Mike on his leash

Kemp (Homeski Skeezer):
I want to wish you luck in school and with the babes. Had fun with the hand-shake. Check you out later, homeboy!

—*Noah (Mr. Fresh)*

To Kemp:
Good luck in H.S. and best wishes. I hope we have fun next year in Murrow.

—*Jessica*

To Kemp:
Have a fun time and good luck. We have something in common, we both hate Allen.

—*Sam G.*

To Kemp:
Old buddy, old pal o' mine. A good friend I knew for a whole year and a half and were like brothers. We shared everything together. I hope our friendship stays like that. Call me up.

—*Your best buddy,*
Henry (Iceman)

• • •

1984, Brooklyn.

I could hear her calling me loud and clear, but I couldn't respond. Acknowledging her now meant turning my attention away from the game, which meant certain doom at the hand of Marvin's dodgeball toss.

"Kempie! Do you hear me? Kempie? Keeeempie!"

Jesus Mom, would you shut the fuck up?

"Hey man, your moms is calling you," Louie says, like I didn't hear her already. I don't respond to his notice, either, as I try to remain focused on Marvin's toss. My concentration doesn't help. He chucks the basketball at me with lightning speed, and before I can even think of what to do, the ball ricochets off my left cheek and sends me sprawling across the floor. Marvin immediately goes into sore winner mode.

"Ha, ha! I got you, bitch!"

I can feel the side of my face swelling already as I coolly try to compose myself. After a few seconds of trying to ignore Marvin's taunts, I step from the courtyard of our building (where we usually play our games of dodgeball) and onto the sidewalk, where I'm now visible to Mom, as she continues to shout from our fifth-floor apartment window.

"Yeah Ma?"

"Time to come up and eat. The food's ready."

I'd originally planned to beg for a few more minutes to play with my friends, but now I saw the demand to come upstairs as a sort of rescue from the humiliation. I knew my friends had heard her, too, so they wouldn't question my sudden exit.

"I've gotta go upstairs now to eat," I say.

"You comin' back out later?" Louie asks.

"Aw, I don't know. Maybe," I reply, by now in a rush to get into the building before the swelling on my face becomes obvious and the real taunts begin. I pull out my set of keys, a gift of responsibility given to me the year before when I entered the fifth grade, and make my hasty exit.

I hurry up the stairs and enter our apartment, 5F. As soon as the door swings open, I catch the smell of the paprika potatoes sizzling on the stove. Mom only whipped up this tasty concoction about one Sunday a month. A simple dish, created by mixing potatoes, a healthy dose of paprika, pepper, salt, and onions into a large pot and frying it in a pan's worth of bacon grease, it was my favorite thing to eat outside the realm of fast food. I couldn't stand too long in the doorway to savor the smell, though, because I had to get into the bathroom and see if my face had swollen up.

"What happened to you?" Mom shouts.

Too late. I know what she's talking about, but try to shrug as though I'm confused.

"Your face! It looks a little swollen."

Getting hurt while playing with friends is a common thing for most kids. However, in the world in which I lived, any injury sustained while participating in unsupervised play was just a reason for Mom to take away one of my neighborhood traveling privileges. And to a sixth-grader with an overprotective mom, that meant Brooklyn would get a lot smaller.

We'd only moved to 224 Hinckley Place a year ago, right before I started the fifth grade. Before that, we lived in an apartment at 470 Ocean Avenue in Flatbush, just a few blocks from the Parkside Avenue entrance to Prospect Park. I was going to P.S. 249 then, and I was so young I wasn't allowed to leave the apartment by myself unless I was going to school. Fortunately, two of my three sisters still lived at home, and they both went to Erasmus High just up the block on Flatbush Avenue, which gave me occasional opportunities to get some air. Unfortunately, my sisters, Sheila (the oldest), Sharon, and Stephany, had always formed a makeshift gang, which meant most trips outside either began or ended with a confrontation with other neighborhood girls.

Things got pretty bad with my sisters' weekly fights. At one point, even my dad, who'd been divorced from my mom since we lived in Coney Island, had to pick up Steph from school after she sliced up another girl's face with a razor blade. The brawls escalated, and it eventually got so bad various neighborhood girls would actually ring the doorbell to our apartment. When my mom answered, they'd speak politely and matter-of-factly, as though they were asking to borrow some sugar: "Miss Powers, this is (fill in the blank with neighborhood girl of choice). Can your daughters come out and fight?"

The pot finally boiled over when someone flung a molotov cocktail at our front door, nearly setting the entire building on fire. I was sitting in the room I shared with my sisters, watching television, when the whole thing happened, and barely noticed the smoke seeping into the apartment, as people screamed and ran around frantically. When the firemen arrived and put out the fire, I thought it was so cool they could carry all of that heavy gear up five flights of stairs. Maybe I'd want to be a fireman one day.

The soot from the blaze covered most of the hallway outside our door. And stayed that way for weeks. This soot also provided Mom with an explanation of why the incident happened: just a few days later, someone scribbled a message into it:

We Know Where You Live Miss Powers

It was addressed to my mom, but it was meant for my sisters. It was time to go.

Hence the move to Hinckley Place, which was only about ten blocks away, but in Brooklyn mileage was virtually a new city. First off, it wasn't in Flatbush, which was almost entirely black. It was in a much more diverse community called Kensington. Hinckley was also the rare Brooklyn street that didn't run endlessly throughout the borough. Instead, it only existed for two blocks, between Stratford Road and East 8th Street, bisected by busy Coney Island Avenue.

Within a year of moving to Hinckley, my sister Sharon had moved out to join the Job Corps, and I was finally coming into my own as an individual, despite still having to share a bedroom with Steph. I'd been given the keys to the apartment, and I suddenly had the freedom to move about the neighborhood for purposes other than going to school, though Mom kept me on a short leash. So short in fact that to me, a map of Brooklyn, New York, pretty much looked like this:

A Map of Brooklyn, New York, 1984
(A.K.A. "WHERE I'M ALLOWED TO GO")
CARTOGRAPHER: KEMP POWERS, II YEARS OLD

Things were happening in New York in 1984. *Big* things. Russell Simmons and Rick Rubin were founding the Def Jam
record label in Rubin's NYU dorm, preparing to popularize the
rap music that had already been the ambient sound in the
background of my childhood. *Purple Rain* hit the theaters that
year, making Prince into as popular an artist as Michael
Jackson. Movies like *Gremlins* were breaking box-office
records and setting new standards for event cinema.

Life and culture were changing in the city and around the
world in profound ways, and I was oblivious to it all. The
crack epidemic was causing one of the most meteoric rises in
crime in the city's history, but those problems never pene-
trated the walls of our little cultural bubble. Crack cocaine?
I couldn't be bothered to think about it. I was too busy
watching Drive-in Theater kung-fu flicks every Saturday
morning and hanging with my friends. There were, of course,
other diversions. For example, I received packs of educational
animal cards every month in the mail. I waited in anticipation
for wolf, Gila monster, and the Komodo dragon cards. I was far
too young to travel to one of the museums in Manhattan, and
Mom didn't have the time to take me there, so the cards were
my own personal natural history collection. I'd read that many
of the animals in my card collection could actually be seen—
in stuffed form anyway—at the Smithsonian Institution. But
the Smithsonian was way down in Washington, D.C., and I
wasn't even allowed off the block.

Cable television was still in its infant stages. Even though
MTV had already been out for several years, the only cable stations Brooklynites were privy to were HBO and WHT. Yeah, I
loved rap music, but the culture of it was too dangerous and I

was too young to be considered a participant. My sisters hung with DJs, and someone was always getting stabbed or shot at a club. For me the lifestyle consisted of rhyming in front of a full-length mirror and stealing copies of my sisters' *Right On!* magazines. My breakdancing skills were limited to only the most basic pop-locking, and my only Wild Styles were in the pages of my composition book or on the window of a subway car when Mom wasn't looking, where I'd scribble my "Pup" tag with a black marker.

For the most part, everything I ever needed or desired (education, entertainment, excitement) could be found within my own small world, which began as soon as I exited our apartment. The courtyard (1) just outside the entrance to our building was the perfect setting for games of dodgeball. Also, since it was out of view and earshot, unless you really screamed, of our apartment window, my friends and I could curse freely and fight without fear of getting caught by Mom (who'd then notify other parents).

Going to the store (2a or 2b) could mean visiting either the little bodega at the corner of Hinckley and Coney Island Avenue, or the Te-Amo newsstand and cigar shop across the street. Mom sent me there at least once a day to buy her essentials: a two-liter bottle of Pepsi and a pack of Winston cigarettes. My sister Stephany was a Newport smoker, but was still deftly hiding it from Mom back then. Te-Amo was also my backup source of comic books when I didn't have time to go to Brain Damage (6). We stopped buying macaroni & cheese or rice from the store when we started finding bugs in the boxes of pasta. About once a month Mom made me redeem huge bags of empty plastic Pepsi bottles for what seemed like spare change. It was an embarrassing ordeal, since there never failed to be one of my friends hanging around when I was walking with the bottles, which resulted in a round of heckling.

To my friends and me, "going to the store" was also synonymous with hanging out all over the neighborhood. For example, if I said, "Ma, I'm going to the store," I could be expected to go first to Louie's house to play Transformers or He-Man, then to Eddie's house and listen to him talk whatever nonsense he was talking that day, then play a quick game of Chinese handball, before actually going anywhere near the store. Fortunately, none of our parents ever questioned why it took us an hour to walk up the block and buy a can of Mello Yello or Nu-Grape.

Unfortunately, in order to get to the store I had to pass by the gated house owned by the corner Nazi (3). The white guy who lived there never spoke. He was bald, with a long goatee that made him look like an outlaw biker. A bigger concern was his very large and very mean bull terrier, which made every effort to jump the fence anytime anyone walked by. Eventually, it had a litter of puppies—meaning there were about six dogs trying to scale the fence and maul me as I passed.

School (4) was P.S. 130 on 70 Ocean Parkway, about a ten-minute walk from our apartment. I transferred from P.S. 249 to this school when we moved to Hinckley Place. The library (5) across the street from school was a regular hangout. I spent most of my time there searching for all of the books I could find on how the world would look in the future. I swore to my friends that Manhattan would be covered by one of Buckminster Fuller's geodesic domes by 2001 to keep out the pollution. I also made it a point never to return any of the books I ever borrowed, a skill picked up from my older sisters.

Brain Damage (6) was the only real comic store in the neighborhood, just outside the Ft. Hamilton Parkway subway station. Carlos, the owner, had a son who went to P.S. 130 with me. That didn't make the surly bastard give any of the kids a break though. Entering the store was like joining the military, with Carlos barking orders at us, like, "no reading books before you buy them!" It was a lot to endure just to buy a lousy comic book. But it was the only place where we could get certain issues, so he was an irritation to be tolerated.

Cheesy Pizza (7), on Caton Avenue, was just a couple of blocks from school, and was the preferred after-school pizza parlor hangout. As the name implies, they also had the cheesiest slices around. Seven Brothers Pizza (8), on Church and Coney Island Avenue, was the pizza parlor I visited to grab slices for Mom or Steph. Not as good as Cheesy Pizza, but closer. Also, "going to get some slices" had basically the same meaning as "going to the store," so a trip to Seven Brothers could be expected to take at least an hour.

The Video Store (9) was further up Coney Island Avenue headed toward the park. The guys who ran this store were cool. Even though the movie you wanted never seemed to be in, they'd hold certain ones for you. The Bike Shop (10) next door was the bigger draw though, at least for my friends and me. We never went here to get stuff for our bikes. We went here because the owner would use the store machinery to drill holes in our quarters for us. Then we'd loop a small piece of thread through the hole and tie the other end to our finger. When playing coin-operated video games, in pizza parlors and outside bodegas all over the neighborhood, we could insert the quarter and pull it right back after the game started. A person with good finger dexterity could get fifteen to twenty-five games from one quarter before the string broke.

Kwong Foo Kitchen (11) was the Chinese take-out place on Church Avenue and East 8th Street. In addition to great shrimp fried rice, they also made tasty fried chicken and french fries. Soon after we arrived, I went to pick up some food from there for Mom. I got hit by a cab while trying to cross the street. Going to school in the weeks after the accident was tough, because my face was covered in scabs and sores. The kids at school were relentless hecklers, but fortunately all of the wounds eventually healed. Despite the accident, Mom also let me continue going here to pick up food—a testament to the quality of their shrimp fried rice.

Eddie's house (12) was across the street from our apartment building. This was one of the rare houses Mom would let me visit unsupervised, probably because Eddie was a smart kid who everyone knew got good grades. Eddie's dad was crazy about his family's German heritage. When his dad wasn't around, Eddie would show me the collector's sword his dad kept, which had a swastika engraved in the handle. He'd then go on to say how if anyone ever came into their house, he could use this sword to poke a hole in their chest. ("Big deal," I'd reply, "my mom's got a gun.") I was happy that Mom let me hang out over here, but sometimes Eddie got on my nerves, especially when he started bragging about all of that Nazi garbage. Once, while we were standing outside of his house, he saw a passing bus full of Hasidic Jewish kids and started singing "Camptown Races," but changed the words to "Hitler had the right idea, doo-dah, doo-dah." Another jackass, and more of a Nazi than the jerk on the corner, but he always kept food in the fridge.

The side of the building (13) was a hangout approved whole-heartedly by Mom. That's because she could see me there just by looking out any of the windows of the apartment. We used the side of the building mostly to play Chinese handball and stickball on mornings before school and on weekends.

Louie's apartment (14) was around the corner on Beverly Road. Louie was my closest friend in the neighborhood. He was Puerto Rican, and his real name was Angel, but everyone (including his mom, dad, and brother) called him Louie. His older brother was mean as hell, but it was still cool to go over to his place and hang for hours at a time. Lou was into the same toys as me, like Transformers, M.A.S.K., and He-Man, so our combined collections were large enough for us to play some great games. His dad and mom were, at least by my adolescent sensibilities, cool, but his mom always seemed to be cooking, while his dad always seemed to be watching soccer on television.

It wasn't like Mom just let me start venturing to all of these places immediately. This map grew slowly during our first year and a half in the building, as she trusted me more and more. When we first got to Hinckley, I wasn't even allowed to cross the street: I'd be taunted by the guys as they sat across from me playing games or eating Italian ices, while all I could do was sit there and give them the finger.

However, any time I got into any kind of trouble, whether or not it was my fault, my map would shrink, as Mom took away a privilege for some unspecified amount of time. "You got hurt riding your bike? Well, I don't want you going around the corner to Louie's house for a while." I couldn't even begin to understand how Mom's mind was working, so it was often better to disguise fights, injuries, or other calamities rather than risk being banned from one of my regular spots.

In other words, there was *no way* I'd admit to the facial swelling while playing a game of dodgeball. That might get me banned from the courtyard.

"I tripped and fell running up the stairs," I reply.

"Oh, well you'd better go put some ice on it," she says. "Go to the bathroom and wash up, then come out here and eat."

Thank goodness.

"And when you're done eating, take that big bag of empty Pepsi bottles to the store."

Shit.

The next morning, the swelling had already gone down and was barely noticeable. I packed my book bag, then headed across the street to knock on Eddie's door. Eddie came out, and we headed over to the side of the building, where we met up with Marvin, Louie, Todd, Dana, and a few of the other guys to play a quick game of Chinese handball before school.

"You know where you're gonna be going to junior high next year?" Eddie asked as we make it to the corner.

"No I haven't really thought about it yet," I replied, thinking it was a little early to be talking about junior high since we were only now closing in on Halloween. Eddie mentioned a really good school in South Brooklyn called Stranahan. I had no idea what he was talking about, but did a good job of faking interest.

I had the little blue ball today, which meant I got to begin the game of handball in the "ace" box. With Chinese handball, any number of kids can play, since each player has a personal court space that consists of a single square of sidewalk. The person in the lead square is the ace, followed by the king, queen, jack, one, two, and so on. The ace always serves the ball down the court. The only rules are that the ball has to bounce once (no more, no less) before hitting the wall. The person who messes up the volley gets booted from his box to the end of the line. The ultimate goal is to get into the ace box and stay there as long as possible.

I managed to stay in the ace box for a respectable number of rounds before I finally got knocked off my perch by Marvin, the neighborhood show off. He regularly bragged about getting to perform in the Big Apple Circus. Our burden of proof was pretty low, so when he sprung into a series of flips and cartwheels, everyone believed his grand claims. Marvin also said he was a master of karate, so he became the de facto bully of the ten- to twelve-year-old set, even though he was shorter than the rest of us.

I languished at or near the end of the line for the rest of the game. Then, my sister Steph stuck her head out of the window.

"It's time to go to school! Get going!" she shouted.

Some of us who'd been sitting in the end boxes started to head toward the street, but Marvin and a couple of the other guys continued to play.

"Gotta go to school," I said to Marvin.

"Go ahead and go," he replied, never taking his eyes off the ball.

"Well, I need my ball," I quietly responded.

"I'll give it to you tomorrow," he said, still not making eye contact.

I looked up at Steph, who was watching patiently. She knew the ball was mine, since she saw me leave the apartment bouncing it.

"Kemp, tell him to give you your ball!" she shouted.

Marvin rolled his eyes and stopped the game. He grabbed the ball and tossed it at me.

"Here! Here's your damn ball, punk!"

I was relieved and started hurrying away. Louie and the rest of the guys seemed to be a little relieved too as I made it to the corner. Then Steph's screaming voice dragged me back into the fray.

"Don't let him talk to you like that!"

I could almost feel Marvin watching me before I even turned around to face him. Suddenly, every kid on the block seemed to be standing around us in a circle. Marvin threw the first kick, one of his fabled karate kicks to the chest. I grabbed his foot, then began spinning him around in a circle. I heard the "oohs" of the crowd, and for a split second thought I might be able to pull this fight off. But instead of falling over, Marvin pulled me in closer and took a couple of whaling swings to my back. I was surprised that they didn't hurt at all, and pushed him back into the grass in front of my building. He charged back, knocking me to the grass with a running tackle. I heard one of the legs of my pants tear as I hit the ground. As I tried to get back up, Marvin jumped onto my back and put me in a headlock. I started to choke.

"That's enough Marvin," Steph shouted down. "Let him up now. You won."

Marvin looked up at Steph, then got up and walked off. I also stood up, too embarrassed to make eye contact with any of the guys.

"Go to school Kemp," Steph shouted.

I looked up at her.

"I can't," I replied. "My pants tore."

By the time I got to school, the word had already spread.

Kemp fought Marvin.

Even though Marvin had always bragged of his many conquests, no one had actually seen him fight. They just took his word he was tough, and stayed out of his way, so my little handball altercation was quite a revelation.

The first person to come up and talk to me about it was Allen. Allen despised me, and I despised him back. His dad was our teacher, and he always made a point of calling on Allen in class and reproaching his wrong answers with almost Dickensian cruelty. I had no idea what that had to do with me, but nonetheless the kid was always harassing me about one thing or another.

"Hey Kemp," he said smiling. "I heard you got into a fight with Marvin."

I quietly complied.

"I heard he beat your ass," Allen continued, elated, "and that he tore your pants off."

"I lost the fight," I replied. "But he didn't tear my pants off. They just ripped when I fell."

"Yeah, right," Allen countered as he walked off. "You got your pants torn off."

I thought it was going to be a long day, with lots of comments like Allen's. I was shocked when the next person to approach me, a girl named Nikki, took a different stance.

"I heard you got into a fight with Marvin," she said.

I once again complied, waiting for her follow-up sarcastic remarks.

"I hate him. He's such an asshole," she said. Then she smiled at me and walked off. Most of the remaining comments of the day were just like hers. More consolation and admiration than ridicule. A couple of girls even told me they "liked" me.

By the time Halloween rolled around, my stature in the neighborhood and at school had increased tremendously. It didn't matter that the only reason I stood up to Marvin was because my sister forced me to. What mattered was that I'd faced him, and even though I'd lost, our fight emboldened everyone in the neighborhood. Suddenly, no one was scared of Marvin. I was far from being the alpha wolf, but I was generally respected as a cool guy instead of the momma's boy I'd been regarded as in years past. I was finally growing up.

Holidays in the neighborhood were an exciting time. While households in other parts of the country might have looked forward to the gifts and food of Christmas and Thanksgiving, our neighborhood really got excited for the lesser holidays. Independence Day, for example, was a time when the neighborhood kids tried their best to blow up the entire block.

Laws regulating fireworks were lax at best, so in the weeks leading up to the holiday weekend we would all begin stockpiling collections of explosives. Because of Mom's watchful eye, my collection was limited to a small assortment of bottle rockets, snakes, and firecrackers. I lived vicariously through my less supervised friends, who described their arsenals by the number of units it would take to constitute a stick of dynamite. For example, according to experts such as Eddie and Marvin, it took about eight "blockbuster" firecrackers to equal one stick of dynamite.

It's a ridiculous assertion now, but back then it seemed totally plausible, especially after being rocked by the sound of a blockbuster going off. Placing them inside soda cans enabled us to create homemade fragmentation grenades, with shrapnel spraying in every direction.

When the Fourth of July hit, Hinckley Place put on a better fireworks show than anything one would see over the East River. The condition of the streets the next day was proof, as a layer of firework confetti blanketed the entire neighborhood. Still, as fun as it was, Independence Day was still only the second best holiday of the year.

Halloween was every city kid's favorite holiday, because it was one of the rare times of the year when we could head out unsupervised at night. The whole neighborhood seemed to be out on those nights. My friends and I mostly trick-or-treated in my building, the houses that lined East 8th Street, and the walk-up buildings on Beverly Road. We couldn't eat any of the candy until we got home and our parents checked it. There were rumors that kids had been poisoned, and any fruit item we were given was immediately pulled and thrown in the garbage by our parents.

While we were trick-or-treating, the older kids generally threw rotten eggs at each other. They'd also load tube socks with wet sand and swat us on the back as they ran by. So far this Halloween, Louie and I had avoided any eggings or sockings. We were chillin' on his front porch, listening to music blaring from the apartments, as crowds gathered all over the neighborhood. Kids were walking around with cans of spray paint and markers, tagging walls, lampposts, and parked vans.

"I can't believe we're gonna be in junior high next year," Louie said.

I hadn't thought about junior high since Eddie brought it up back when I fought Marvin.

"Yeah," I replied, "it's not that big a deal though. We'll still hang out."

"Not as much as now." He sounded a little sad. "We're gonna have to start riding the subway, and our schools are gonna be far apart."

I hadn't thought of the distances before. I also hadn't considered having to ride the subway to school. I'd never ridden it by myself.

"Well, we'll still make time to hang out," I said. "And besides, we've got this whole summer to hang. It's gonna be fresh!"

A smile came across Louie's face as he realized this summer both of us would have more freedom to roam than we'd ever imagined. It *was* going to be fresh.

Just then, a group of kids ran by, chucking eggs at one another and laughing. One of the eggs splattered a parked motorcycle.

"Hey you fuckin' kid!!!!" The voice rumbled from a neighboring porch, causing the kids to freeze in their tracks. A Puerto Rican guy in his late twenties walked over.

"You like throwin' eggs on other people's shit?"

They shook their heads "NO" in quiet unison. The guy

wasn't satisfied. He pointed to the open carton of eggs in one of the kids' hands.

"Let me see that," he ordered.

The kid handed him the carton. He pulled out a couple of the eggs and examined them for a second. Then he smashed them in the kid's face. The crying kid and his friends ran off, but they stopped at the corner. The egg recipient turned back to the older guy.

"I'm gonna get my brother to come fuck you up!"

The older guy laughed. "Tell him I'll be here all fuckin' night!"

Halloween is fresh.

I never watched the news or read newspapers. All of my reading consisted of copies of Marvel comic books, which I kept sealed in individual plastic bags that I bought from Brain Damage. But starting in late December, things began to change. It was the first time my family had ever gotten into a routine of discussing the news.

Some crazy white guy was on television. His name was Bernard Goetz. He'd just confessed to shooting a bunch of kids on a Manhattan subway car. I was surprised that a white guy had the guts to shoot a bunch of black kids. It's not like this Goetz guy was Italian or anything. Italian guys were tough. Goetz was a geeky-looking guy with thick glasses.

"He said it was in self-defense," my mom remarked. Steph countered immediately.

"But he went back and shot one of the kids again!"

She pointed out a *Daily News* article that had diagrams of

Goetz and how he fired at the four kids on the subway car. Goetz said they were trying to rob him. The kids were saying they'd just "asked him for some money." Yeah, right. If a posse of four older kids asked me for some money, I'd assume I was getting robbed and give it up before one of them stabbed me.

And that was the source of this unusually lively discussion in our household and others' across the city. Lots of people in New York thought Goetz was a hero for standing up to the kids and giving them a taste of their own medicine. I admit, I was pretty petrified to ride the subway, even though I was with my mom and my sisters all of the time. At night, after the regular commuters had returned home, the subway lines that ran deep into Brooklyn were always eerily devoid of life. It seemed like the only people there were bums and delinquent kids. And graffiti was *everywhere*. Most of it wasn't cool like the stuff Ramo did in the movie *Beat Street*. Maybe the pretty graf was only on the trains that ran in the Bronx. In Brooklyn, it was mostly black marker scribble that covered so much of the trains you sometimes couldn't see out of the windows. There were also puddles of piss everywhere.

Standing up to kid thieves was one thing. But the fact that this Goetz guy had actually gone back and shot one of them again, even going so far as to tell him, "you seem to be doing all right, here's another," really incensed a lot of people. I wasn't one of them. I thought what he did was some cool, Charles Bronson, *Death Wish*-style move. That would be great, if one of those kids from Erasmus tried to stop me on the train and I could say something like, "you seem to be doing all right, here's another," after shooting him.

Part of the reason the entire world for my friends and me was encapsulated in just a couple of blocks was because older kids were dangerous. And they seemed to be everywhere. It was like they had a radar that told them when someone was walking alone—that person would suddenly get jumped. They stole my mom's last two cars, including the Grand Prix I loved so much. And it was because of them we could never wear any of the dope gear we wanted. A sheepskin coat or triple-fat goose down jacket would be pulled off of your back before you could make it to school. We had all stopped wearing Lee jeans, because a rumor had begun to circulate around the city that you could trade in the large leather Lee patches from jeans for merchandise like sneakers. Soon, kids were having the Lee patches ripped from their pants on a regular basis. Put up a fight, and you caught the beatdown of your life, from kids just like the ones who tried to jump Goetz. As far as I was concerned, those kids got what they deserved.

● ● ●

The Goetz shooting was probably my friends' and my first time becoming aware of life outside of our neighborhood. The "subway vigilante," as he was called, was heralded as a hero for defending himself from what many saw as a violent and sadistic underclass that was dragging New York City into the dark ages. It started in the seventies, when I was far too young to have any idea what was happening in the world outside of the walls of our apartment. While I was mustering up the courage to eat my first slice of pizza and step into the open sewer that was the Atlantic Ocean, articles were being written about the gang society that had a stranglehold on the city.

According to those articles, roving bands of teenagers had taken over entire neighborhoods, from the farthest reaches of Brooklyn to the northern tip of the Bronx. Technically, there were only about a thousand known gang members in the city by the eighties, down from the reported twenty thousand or more who roamed the streets in the early seventies. Most crimes now were being committed by small posses of crooks with no particular ultimate goal in mind. This made the nature of their crimes much more random, and much more ominous. You couldn't identify your attacker by some gang version of a letter jacket. Every teenager was a potential threat.

Why, then, were we all so attached to Brooklyn? I can't speak for my group of friends, but for me it was because the other option was even worse. The only time I ever left the city was during the summer months, when Mom would send my sisters and me down south to stay with relatives. It's important to understand that every black person in New York City in the eighties who wasn't from the Caribbean seemed to be only one or two generations removed from North Carolina. What Chicago and Detroit were to the legions of migratory blacks from Mississippi, Arkansas, and Louisiana, New York was to black people from North Carolina.

We all still had relatives there. In fact, my sisters and I had inherited land in Roanoke Rapids, North Carolina, a small town near the North Carolina/Virginia border. It was the only place I'd been outside of the city, despite my efforts. I'd tried on several occasions to convince Mom during the drives down to stop for a day in Washington, D.C. The Smithsonian Institution was there, and it seemed like every artifact, exhibit, or work of art I'd ever read about was located there. The answer from Mom was always no, and I'd grown accustomed to seeing the tip of the Washington Monument off in the distance as we crossed the Potomac on Interstate 95, knowing that that was as close to the Smithsonian as I'd ever get. It was a somber yearly routine. Mom would send us all down to North Carolina for summers to escape the pressure cooker atmosphere of the city, but my sisters, much older and much smarter, would always do something to get sent right back home within the first week. Steph would get sassy and talk back to one of the adults. Sharon would disobey directions and set up permanent residence on the living room sofa. It was like they devised their plan of transgression before they even arrived. Within days, the telephone call would be made.

"I can't handle these girls. They don't know how to listen. I think I need to send them home. But little Kempie can stay. He's a good one."

By the time I'd finished unpacking my clothes, my sisters were gone. They were back in Brooklyn, enjoying the bulk of summer vacation with friends, opening fire hydrants, and running the neighborhood, while I was left alone with my aunt Martha and uncle Buddy in the sticks.

What might have seemed like a natural paradise to others was an oppressive hell for me, and Aunt Martha was its gatekeeper. They lived on a small farm, and all of the meals were grown on the land, from corn to cabbage. It sounds nice now, but for a kid raised on McDonald's and fiending for some fries like crack, it was a culinary nightmare. When we went into town to go to the store, I'd be allowed to buy one bag of Cheez Doodles. When we got back to the house, Martha would empty the bag into a kitchen drawer, then explain how I'd be given a few doodles for every chore I completed.

To top it off, there was no bathroom in their house. I was forced to wash in a large basin Martha would place in her living room. She'd pour hot water into the basin, then call me into the room naked to get in. Going to the bathroom at night was a test of courage, as the trip to the outhouse involved battles with bugs and snakes. Once, I even made the mistake of looking down into the stall before going, and the writhing mass of worms I saw at the bottom made me afraid to sit on a toilet seat for weeks. It's no wonder I never wanted to leave the city, when *this* was what the outside world looked like to me. I'd take my chances on the streets of Brooklyn any day.

By the time I'd reached adolescence, I'd been trained to fear the city's society of violence, even though I'd never actually encountered it. Sure, my friends and I would jostle with other subway riders and engage in loud, often profane conversations while walking down the street, but we weren't any danger to anyone. Every last one of us was an honor student, among the best and brightest in our class. We were encouraged by our teachers to be successful, and we argued over who would be accepted into Harvard and who would go to Princeton or some other Ivy League school. The murder rate in the city ballooned to more than two thousand per year, yet we remained about as clueless about the crime problem as any reasonable human could be. Smart people, we thought, knew where they should and shouldn't go.

Bernard Goetz changed all of that. Before then, I hadn't even noticed the racially mixed nature of my crew of friends. We were black, white, Chinese, Eastern European, Puerto Rican.

But to the city whose hidden rage was metastasized by the Goetz incident, we were all just different flavors of the same problem. It hit me squarely in the face shortly after the Goetz incident, when I was going to the store for my mother.

I was about to turn the corner when a deep voice called out to me. I turned to see a man motioning to me from across the street. He trotted over to my side as though he had to tell me something. I thought maybe I'd dropped something and this guy was, amazingly, about to give it back.

"Hey man," he said. This guy was tall. He looked to be about twenty-five or so. He appeared to be Puerto Rican.

"What's up?" I replied, trying to play it as cool as possible. That's when things went bad.

"Come here!" he shouted, suddenly enraged as he grabbed me by the arm. I was so shocked I didn't know what to do. I'd never even seen this fuming ogre before, so what did he want from me?

He dragged me over to a fence, then pulled out a pair of silver handcuffs. Was he a cop? He slapped one side of the handcuffs around a fence and slapped the other side tightly on my wrist. I was starting to panic, but up to this point I hadn't let out a single sound. He stepped back and stared at me, smiling.

"You like that?" he asked.

I could feel the tears welling up in my eyes, and finally opened my mouth to respond.

"Man, what did I do?"

That's when he really got angry. He started rambling about how he knew I was up to no good. How all of the little bastards like me were dragging the city down into the gutter. He said he should kill me like Goetz killed those bastards on the subway. Or that he should leave me cuffed to that fence to rot.

The sound of all of this was too much, and the tears rolled down my cheeks. He stood there for a few seconds, just laughing at me, then finally came over and removed the handcuffs.

"Get the fuck out of here," he said, pushing me nearly to the ground and then walking away. I got up and wiped off my face. The corner Nazi's bull terrier had witnessed the entire scene, but sat there strangely quiet, looking at me. I continued on to the store, then went home, never mentioning it to my mother. But inside, I'd finally realized I was seen as one of those terrible kids the city hated so much.

I couldn't understand how it happened. My friends and I rarely did anything that didn't involve Chinese handball, comic books, or bikes. We didn't even want to bother with girls, so why would any woman be scared of us raping her? I sat there that afternoon going over it in my mind.

I watched a cockroach standing on the wall, its feelers slowly waving back and forth. Mom inched closer to it from behind. Just as she raised her shoe to smash the bug, it skittered across the wall and behind a picture frame. Mom gave chase, just missing it with a swat as it zipped behind the frame, only leaving the black smudge mark from the shoe on the wall.

She sighed, put the shoe down, and grabbed the edges of the picture frame to take it down and expose the little intruder. I turned my attention back to the comic book I'd pulled out. Mom lowered the picture frame from the wall to reveal about a hundred roaches, the collective forming the exact square shape of the picture frame. She shrieked as the roach square exploded in every direction, little brown streaks heading behind cabinets, chairs, and the television. Within a matter of seconds, they were all gone, leaving only the small dots of their droppings stuck to the wall as proof of their presence.

Mom cursed as she stormed out of the room. I stayed there, continuing to read my comic book. The roaches were filthy and I hated them too. They made nests in my Tyco racetracks and I had to throw them out. They had infested our entire building. But for the world around me, there was another infestation going on, and unfortunately, I was seen as the vermin.

Part Two.

When junior high school began, everything suddenly changed. At Eddie's suggestion, I'd decided I wanted to go to a junior high in South Brooklyn called Stranahan, or J.H.S. 142. Every school in New York City has a number delineation as well as a name, and many of them are recognized more for their number than their name. I never knew what the names of P.S. 130 or P.S. 249 were when I was attending them. I just knew their numbers. Eddie and his parents said 142 had a great magnet program that was known for placing kids in some of the city's elite high schools—the educational Shangri-Las of Brooklyn Tech, Bronx Science, Hunter College High, and (gasp!) even Stuyvesant, the top-rated public high school in New York City.

If teenagers today are overly anxious about making the right college choice and the impact it'll have on their lives, they'd be amazed to know a similar anxiety affects New York City school kids beginning as early as elementary school. We were all public school students. Even those of us whose parents were home-owners (a ridiculous rarity) could not afford private school. We had to navigate a virtual minefield, beginning in junior high, to go to the right school in order to assure our success in life.

Making the right decision wasn't easy. The city had an open enrollment policy for junior high and high school students, meaning students in any borough could apply to any school in the city, as long as they were willing to spend time traveling on the subway to get there. We received large catalogues near the end of our elementary and junior high years that laid out all of the schools in the city, as well as their areas of specialization. Whether or not you got into the school of your choice was determined by a combination of seats available and your scores on citywide reading and math exams. This was where our little crew shined, as almost every one of us regularly scored in the top two percent citywide on those exams, giving us free choice of some of the best schools.

And if you didn't get into the school of your choice? Well, you could always go to your zone school. For some, this wasn't such a bad thing. But for us, living in a border neighborhood, it meant we'd be forced to attend schools where criminals outnumbered students. I'd learned enough from hearing my sisters recount tales of brawls and razor duels at Erasmus to know I wanted no part of it.

It wasn't like you were off the hook even if you attended one of the better schools. Once again, the fact that every school must admit all children residing in a nearby zone meant that even the elite schools had a pretty sizable knucklehead contingent: thugs from the neighborhood who are just there to intimidate and rob other kids. The city's answer to this mixing of student types was then and still is today the magnet program. The magnet program is a series of "advanced learning" classes within the school that forms a kind of upper educational caste. Magnet students take only magnet classes with other students, having almost no interaction with the rest of the student body. Even within the magnets, there is a ranking system, from M(agnet)-1 through M-3, with M-1 being the kids who score the highest on the standardized tests. A poor performance on any of the seasonal exams can get a student dropped from one magnet to another. A really poor performance can even get a kid dropped out of the magnet program altogether and into the "regular" classes, a death sentence if ever there was one.

So I made the decision to attend Stranahan, which immediately concerned Mom. The school's location in South Brooklyn meant that I'd have to take a twenty-minute subway ride on the F train from the nearby Fort Hamilton Parkway stop all the way to the Carroll Street station. Up until this point, I had never been allowed to ride the subway by myself, and Mom wasn't exactly thrilled that her twelve-year-old would be making a daily rush-hour commute.

As it turned out, Eddie wasn't the only other person from P.S. 130 who decided to attend 142. Several of the girls from my class had also chosen the school, and their mothers, equally concerned about the new subway experience, chipped in and rented a van service to shuttle them to school in the morning. My mom liked the idea, and paid for me to take the van ride also.

Now, there have been moments of embarrassment in my life. I've been rejected by girls, lost fights, been singled out for making stupid comments, you name it. But to this day, I cannot recall a more embarrassing moment than stepping out of that van the first day of school, a black guy surrounded by several shy little Jewish girls (Eddie had the foresight to take his chances on the subway). The school was bustling with activity as the van pulled up, and when the door swung open and we stepped out, it was as though the entire student body froze and watched us exit the van. I could read the "what the fucks?" on every face. I began riding the subway the very next day.

It was amazing just how fast my old friendships faded. With the exception of Eddie, all of the guys from the neighborhood went to different schools, and within a couple of weeks of that first day, it seemed like I was only seeing them on rare occasions. The replacements came fast and easy, though. I quickly struck up friendships with several people in my M-1 class, including Mack, the only other black guy. Mack was about as dark as the chalkboard, but he had an Italian last name. He explained that one of his earlier relatives was Italian. Mack introduced me to two of his old neighborhood friends. Edwin was also in our class. A thin Puerto Rican kid, he was an aspiring artist who seemed to be better groomed than any of the girls in our class. He would be singled out as a homosexual within months.

"By the way, his older sister's fine as hell," Mack would remind me repeatedly.

Mack's other elementary school friend wasn't even in our class, but became part of our little crew anyway. Henry was in M-3, and his family had known Mack's for a while. He was more built than the rest of us, but you couldn't tell because he wore a long black trench coat. He wasn't an intimidating guy, though. In fact, he was quite the opposite, always sporting a warm smile.

Several other friends followed. Mike was also in my class,

but we didn't become friends until we had our first confrontation. After school one day, I found a five-dollar bill lying on the sidewalk and quickly claimed it. Mike pointed out that the bill was dropped by Jesse, another of our classmates, and that I should return it. Mike was one of the shortest kids I had ever seen, so I told him outright to fuck off. He pushed the subject, even telling Jesse to get his money back from me. Jesse refused when I gave him a cold stare, but Mike kept on going, pointing out how wrong I was. I thought it was cool that the little guy would stand up to someone so much bigger, so we started hanging out after that. But I kept the five bucks.

These and other friendships came over the course of several weeks, and several of us took to walking to the subway station together after school. Still, those first few days of riding the subway were very lonely ones. I was usually half-asleep when I first hopped onto the F train for my new morning commute. My eyes never fully came into focus until the train erupted from the dark subway tunnel and climbed high above the city streets to stop at the Smith-9th Street station, just before Carroll Street and school. There were always large groups of students gathered on this platform, taking in some of the city air in the shadow of the large Kentile Floors sign. Guys were running around, feeling up girls' asses. Commuters were trying their best to ignore the throngs of teens, burying their faces into their newspapers and hoping one of the kids didn't inadvertently trample them.

There were only five stops between home and school, but it was like I was traveling into a different world. Stranahan sat on the geographic border of two very different neighborhoods, physically divided by a sudden turn in the Gowanus

Expressway. On one side, there was Carroll Gardens, a firmly entrenched neighborhood of brownstones populated almost entirely by Italians. On the other side was Red Hook, a neighborhood composed largely of blacks and Puerto Ricans, which also contained several housing projects. As luck would have it, Stranahan was the zone school for both neighborhoods. The fights between black and Italian students started almost on the first day. Both sides had their alpha dogs. I have no idea who the *enfant terrible* of the Italian kids was, but on the black side there was no doubt whom you wanted to avoid.

Butchy was short. *Really* short. I was about 5'8" by now, and when standing next to him, his head never seemed to rise higher than my neck. Perhaps that's why it was lost on me why this kid seemed to lead a squadron of thugs from Red Hook who towered over us more than any of the teachers. If you passed him in the halls, you didn't make eye contact. If Butchy decided he wanted to "snuff" you, you just got snuffed that day. Your best bet was to pretend he was a little grizzly bear and play dead. That was the unfortunate fate that befell Ralph, one of the kids in my M-1 class, shortly after school began. Butchy cornered Ralph on a staircase and slapped him across his face. The rest of us watched in mute horror, but couldn't do anything to help Ralph, or else we too would be on the receiving end of a demoralizing bitch slap.

It was a rare interaction, and just a fact of life for all of us. Everyone was one of two social classes: those jumping people or those getting jumped. The magnet kids liked to think of ourselves as a third, more evasive class. Navigating the minefield from the front door of your apartment building to your classroom took a combination of skills both physical and mental.

Butchy was just one of many physical roadblocks on the path to education that began long before I stepped through the doors of Stranahan.

The subway was an altogether different challenge. Within a couple of weeks, we'd already begun to ride the train in fairly large groups when school let out, but that was far from a guarantee of not being accosted. The platform itself made everyone a target, as kids from other schools (as well as the special education students from Stranahan) took to riding between the subway cars. As they accelerated out of the station on their train, they'd toss things back at us standing on the platform. Their projectile of choice was large D-cell batteries. Some days we looked like ballerinas, twirling and dodging on the platform as the batteries whizzed by our heads and cracked loudly against the walls behind us. After a while, battery dodging became second nature. You learned where to stand on the platform so as not to be in the line of fire when they came hurtling in your direction. My personal preference was near the entrance to the platform, on a set of benches by the turnstile. It didn't put me completely out of harm's way, but since this was also the area where commuters entered the station, picking my head out of the crowd to target would be like finding a chocolate-covered "Where's Waldo?" The other option was at the rear end of the platform, out of the range of any projectiles, but also far from where most of the other kids were standing.

Still, despite these and other distractions, that first year at Stranahan was a liberating one. I developed a series of routines and learned of hangouts that were far from the borders of my small elementary school world. Everyone at school who didn't have a taste for the rotten cafeteria food would simply wander off of campus during lunch. Some would go home, if they lived nearby, but most would head across the street to "the Dungeon," a basement deli that sold cheap one-dollar hero sandwiches to the students. The owner was able to keep the prices so low by skimping on the ingredients. Particularly the meat. If you bought a turkey and cheese sandwich, you could almost mistake the turkey for a mild seasoning, so little of it was present. Still, only paying a dollar made us feel like we were getting an amazing deal, something that rarely occurred in Brooklyn.

The film that best tapped into the zeitgeist back then was *Red Dawn*, a cheesy action flick starring Patrick Swayze as the leader of a group of teenagers who rebel when the Russian Army invades the United States. We had all decided that an invasion and/or nuclear war was definitely in our immediate future, and exchanged info about which of our apartment buildings were equipped with basement fallout bomb shelters and where we'd meet when the machine guns and nuclear winter came. We were regular readers of *Soldier of Fortune*, the accepted magazine of mercenaries and contract killers the world over, but were disappointed to see that every gun and bladed weapon in the catalogues was available for delivery anywhere in the United States "except New York and New Jersey." I pointed out how my mom had several guns, and that my place would probably be the best choice, since the fabricated weapons in books like *The Poor Man's James Bond* or *The Anarchist's Cookbook* would be virtually useless in a war-type scenario. Honestly, who was going to take down a Russian soldier with a homemade zip gun?

• • •

"Do you know what Howard Beach is?"

I stood there frozen for a moment, unsure of how to answer the question. Of course I knew what Howard Beach was. I hadn't before, because I'd only been to Queens once, but Howard Beach could have been one of any endless number of Italian neighborhoods scattered throughout the five boroughs. Places where black people were not welcome. Places like Bensonhurst and Bay Ridge. Even Carroll Gardens, when school was out, wasn't exactly a very welcoming place for black and Puerto Rican kids either. Now, thanks to Howard Beach, it was downright hostile.

Yeah, I know what Howard Beach is.

The Italian kid stares at me for several more seconds, sizing me up. His three friends stand around me in a half-circle, waiting for his command to pounce. He thinks about it for a bit, then a smirk comes across his face.

"Good. You better not fuckin' forget it either."

He motions to his wingmen, and the crew wanders off, leaving me to complete my lunchtime trip to the candy store. Things got so bad so quickly in and around school, it was shocking. And things had been going so well. Seventh grade had gotten off to a rocky start at Stranahan, but things had calmed down by the end of that year. My crew of new friends quickly grew. Mack ended up getting moved from M-1 down to M-3, but we still hung out every day, along with Henry, Mike, Joe, Edwin, Chris, and others. I even got to take my first trip out of the city to someplace other than North Carolina that year when we had our class trip to Disney World. It was my first time on an airplane, and the days at Disney and Epcot Center were more magical than anything I'd seen in any commercial.

The rivalry between the magnet classes was pretty intense early on. Being in M-1, we thought of ourselves as naturally superior to our rivals in M-2 and M-3. Our consistently excellent citywide test scores proved it. We were brought crashing down to Earth during a boroughwide reading of William Shakespeare's *The Tempest*. After several public schools attended a performance of the play, we were charged with re-enacting certain scenes at the large amphitheater in Prospect Park. From Stranahan, M-1 and M-3 would each do a scene. We practiced liberally in class by reading from our script, confident that the audience would be impressed by our able handling of the Shakespearean language. Unfortunately for us, M-3 got to go on first. Before the actors entered, several students from the class, including Mack, came onto the stage and began to provide sound effects into the microphone. Out limped Johnny, completely naked except for a mask and a large man-diaper, as Caliban.

Holy shit. These guys not only had their lines memorized, but they were wearing costumes! By the time the standing ovation for the performance had ended, and Mark, two girls from our class, and I took to the stage to do our scene, costumeless, we were completely shaken. We tried to read from our scripts, since we never bothered to memorize anything, and repeatedly flubbed our lines because of our uniform stage fright. Our teacher was absolutely no help, standing just offstage, prodding us to continue. It was all her fault. When we asked if we should memorize our lines, she brushed the suggestion off and said, "don't worry about it." Why *would* she worry? She was nestled safely in the crowd, just another witness to our verbal butchery of one of the classics. Despite my love of Shakespeare, it was so demoralizing I wouldn't sit through a production of *The Tempest* again until I saw a Royal Shakespeare Theatre performance at the Barbican in London . . . when I was twenty-four years old.

The episode did, however, inspire a newfound respect in M-1 for M-3, and the three classes mingled much better thereafter. We were beginning to come into our own not only as individuals, but as a group. We were no longer on the periphery of teen Brooklyn culture, but we were a part of it. When a Burger King promotional campaign promised cash and prizes to any contestant who could spot the nerdy-looking character "Herb" walking into a local restaurant, we took to shouting the trademark "I found Herb!" every time we wanted to point someone out as being a nerd. By the end of the year, every kid in Brooklyn had taken to calling punks and nerds "Herbs," and the term has stuck around to this very day.

I even overcame my fear of the country instilled in me by my aunt Martha, thanks to Jesse, a classmate whose dad invited me one weekend to go apple picking with them. The idea, to my adolescent sensibilities, seemed so "gay" I wanted to beat myself up, but it was a revelation traveling out of the city and going someplace where I could pick something off of a tree, eat it, and not need a tetanus shot. During our class trip to the Poconos in Pennsylvania, when the woodland guide told us the water from the streams was clean enough to drink, we all dunked our faces into the clear brook and gulped down about a gallon each.

The only blemish on the year was the midterm transfer of Allen, my old nemesis from P.S. 130, to 142. I never knew why the kid didn't like me back then, but whatever his reasons, that animosity picked right back up when he arrived at Stranahan. He and Mack were at each other's throats almost immediately. They got into a brief after-school fight once, where Allen's spinning, twirling karate kicks drew an excited shout from the assembled crowd of "the Karate Kid!" None of the kicks connected with Mack, who eventually moved in and got into a grappling contest with him. Mack backed him against a car, looked into his eyes and blew him a kiss.

Allen took the conflict to a new level when he paid Butchy to harass Mack between classes. One of Butchy's minions smacked Mack on the back of the head with a notebook. Mack, obeying the tried and true rule of not making eye contact with the little grizzly or his pack, continued walking, ignoring their chants. His lack of interest caused Butchy's crew to back off, and Allen seethed in the background. He knew he wasn't getting his money back for the half-hearted bumrush. Later on I found out the reason Allen harbored such a disdain for me, and anyone who called himself my friend: a girl he had a crush on back at 130 rejected him because she had a crush on me. I was clueless the entire time, as I was too busy trying to find a pen pal in Australia, but he'd resented me ever since.

But now Allen was in the same boat as all of the black kids in Stranahan's magnet program. We were finding ourselves in the midst of what was degenerating into a race war. And not just in South Brooklyn, but across the entire city. It all started on December 20, 1986, when the car of twenty-three-year-old Michael Griffiths and his friends, Cedric Sandiford and Timothy Grimes, broke down in Howard Beach, Queens. They walked into a neighborhood pizza parlor to use a telephone and were greeted with hostility by the owners. While they sat and ate pizza, a mob quietly formed to deal with the black trespassers in the neighborhood. When the trio left the pizza parlor, they were attacked. Griffith and Sandiford were beaten senseless by the mob, which wielded baseball bats and tree limbs as weapons, while Grimes managed to escape by fleeing through a hole in a fence onto the busy Shore Parkway. A rapidly approaching automobile struck and killed him—and set off a racial firestorm across the city. The Howard Beach case became one of the first race-bias cases in New York to gain national attention.

The fact was, every Italian neighborhood in the borough had an unofficial gang composed of the teens who lived there. The only purpose of these gangs seemed to be intimidating visitors who weren't Italian. Carroll Gardens already had the South Brooklyn Boys. Then there were the Kings Highway Boys, who hung around Kings Highway near McDonald Avenue and took to shaving the initials "KHB" into the sides of their heads. The Bay Parkway Boys were another street-centric crew. But they might as well have all been the same gang. These communities always saw themselves as outposts in danger of being invaded, with blacks and Puerto Ricans playing the role of Mongol horde. Part of the reason there was so much peace at Stranahan was because the racial contingents were equal in size, keeping each other at bay with the threat of mutually assured destruction.

But Howard Beach was a rallying call for the neighborhood's Italian Americans to unite against the blacks and Puerto Ricans of neighboring Red Hook. Suddenly, sideways glances that would have in the past been ignored erupted into full-blown brawls in the halls and on the streets.

Our little crew found itself in a very awkward position. We were all different races. Mack and I were black. Henry and Edwin were Puerto Rican. Mike, Jared, and Joe were Italian. Chris and Kenny were Chinese. Mark was Jewish. Jesse, Billy, and Geoff were plain old white kids. Nobody knew what on Earth Ralph was. In just a year, we'd established friendships with kids from different factions at the school, and everyone was getting along. Even Butchy warmed up to Mack and laid off of us by now. Within a week of Howard Beach, we were longing for the good old days of being assaulted by the kids from John Jay on Halloween. The menace in the neighborhood was palpable, and it wasn't just coming from teenagers. The adults sat on their porches as we walked to the subway station after school, often taunting us with chants of "Howard Beach" as their wives and mothers leaned out of their windows and nodded in approval.

The fights at and near school became a regular occurrence. At least twice a week I'd arrive in class to hear Joe or Mario telling some tale about an after hours brawl between the guys in the neighborhood and the kids from Red Hook who dared to try crossing the bridge that connected the two neighborhoods. Their friends in the neighborhood seemed oblivious to our multicultural group when they'd approach them during lunch or after school and tell them how a friend, be it Joey or Tony or someone else, just got jumped "by some niggers," and motioned them to come and get ready for a fight.

For the first time, many of us were being faced with a danger we weren't equipped to handle. Of course, there were dangers we were accustomed to—that's what made us Brooklyn kids. But dealing with the problems of the streets had always seemed within reason. There was a huge difference between dodging a battery or evading a water balloon filled with Nair and running from an armed mob hoping to kill you. Protection suddenly became the year's theme, and from our little pool of magnet students we decided to form our own little makeshift gang. We called ourselves the K.A.H.T. Corps. It stood for Kids Against Hostile Thugs, but in reality, none of us could stand against anything. Basically, our unofficial manifesto declared that if one of us was getting jumped, the others wouldn't abandon him, but nobody really believed anyone would defend his friends like in some movie. Mack even outright admitted it.

"If y'all are getting jumped, I'm gonna have to run," he said during a walk to the subway one day. Maybe just having the false sense that we belonged to something bigger created an emotional security blanket for us. On paper, we seemed pretty intimidating. We had Henry, a big, strong guy who could fight off kids several years older than him. Mike, despite his diminutive stature, had an older brother, Rocco, who resembled the extras in *Pumping Iron*. Mack, even being an admitted deserter, was a pretty big guy also. And then we had me. What did I have to contribute? Well, in a worst-case scenario, I knew where Mom kept several handguns hidden around the house.

● ● ●

A gun meant power. Nowhere was this more the case than in New York, where the restrictions on firearms meant only the most hardcore thugs had one. If a kid had access to a .22 pistol, he was a straight-up gangster. The only people I knew who had a firearm were the Jamaican drug dealers who roamed Flatbush Avenue in the late hours of the night. In places like North Carolina, it was possible to walk into just about any store in town and buy the gun of your choice. Uncle Buddy actually kept several rifles and shotguns propped up against the wall in his kitchen, right next to the broom and dustpan, in case he had to run outside and shoot a snake. There wasn't a single store I knew of in the city that sold guns, and that made them even more iconic. A gun alleviated the need to roll ten or twenty people deep when venturing out at night. The sight of a polished pistol handle would turn away some kid who might not be dissuaded by a switchblade or a butterfly knife.

I knew guns like I knew comic books. The names, the calibers, the ammo count in a clip. The Calico M-100 was a .22 caliber pistol, but it's unusual bullpup design allowed a clip that could hold one hundred bullets. The recoil on the .45 caliber pistol made it difficult to aim, but if you nailed your target, it had the stopping power that a .38 could never match. Our long, rambling conversations about firearms garnered me a reputation as a gun nut as I left Stranahan. I saw them as works of art. I saw them as ingenious mechanic tools.

Oddly enough, the one thing I never associated guns with was death. Despite the danger and turmoil that was a routine part of city life, I'd never actually been directly exposed to death. Our very first group encounter with death came in the waning months of our final year at Stranahan, when Pat, a friend of Joe's who was a grade below us, died unexpectedly. Even then, his death came not as a result of violence, but because of reckless driving.

Pat and a group of friends piled into another person's car to go joyriding one night. The driver lost control of his car and plowed into the back of a flatbed truck, killing Pat and several others, some of whom were completely dismembered. Only the driver survived, and he was under constant suicide watch.

By the time ninth grade started, Pat's death seemed like a distant memory. And things were looking up in general. It was time once again to break up the crew, this time for the transition into high school. I had made my school selection long before most other students my age. Edward R. Murrow High School sat in the middle of the Midwood section of Brooklyn, on Avenue L just off of Coney Island Avenue. Murrow was unique among the city's high schools for several reasons. First, the school didn't have any sports teams. Though a football field sat across the street from Murrow's front door, the field was owned by nearby Midwood High. Murrow simply used the field for physical education classes.

Instead, the school sank an inordinate amount of money into a theater and journalism program. We were told the NBC studio next door was where production on *The Cosby Show* was done, and the nearby coffee shop where students went for lunch had walls littered with signed celebrity photographs to emphasize the fact. Murrow's elaborate theater program consisted of several large productions every year. With a budget that went well into the thousands, a Murrow theater production was akin, almost, to what you'd see on Broadway. The students took it seriously, and ticket prices for Murrow shows like *Man of La Mancha* or *Cabaret* were considered steep for kids who were only accustomed to buying tickets to movies.

I personally didn't mind paying the prices, as I'd been enamored with theater ever since Mom took me to see my first Broadway production. It was *La Cage Aux Folles*, and once I got past the fact that it was a story about a bunch of gay guys, I really became overwhelmed by the spectacle of the show. The moving components of the stage that, when combined with the perfect lighting, could emulate a person walking down a busy city street without the use of pricey special effects. Before that, I thought theater was only dramatic plays spoken in a version of English I could only barely comprehend. That show taught me that theater could be as funny and entertaining as anything on a movie screen. I had no desire to perform in a play, but watching one was high entertainment. For having so much invested in the medium, Murrow was a step above most of the other options. But there was more to the place than plays.

There was even a planetarium in the school, one of only two school-based planetariums in the entire city. But this and other bells and whistles paled in comparison to Murrow's unique student culture. Increasingly, high school students across the city were dealing with an experience not unlike venturing into a prison: security guards and metal detectors were part of the morning routine. Murrow was the exact opposite. Students enjoyed a freedom not unlike what one would see on a college campus.

Our homeroom met only once, on the first day of school, where a teacher explained Murrow's unique setup. There was a language we needed to learn to describe our classes and routing. At Murrow, a class period was referred to as a Band. A free period was known as an Opta, and numbers were replaced with letters. Therefore, if the first period of your day was free, you would say that you had an "A-Band Opta." Instead of two semesters, there were four quarters of classes, and we were given free reign to select those classes from an extensive list. There was a set number of credits every student needed to graduate, but how he got to that number was up to him. There were no lunch periods, only Optas. You began as a freshman with two Optas per day, but gained additional ones as you met educational requirements. Liked sleeping in? Schedule your two Optas as the first two Bands of the day and you didn't need to be at school until ten AM. Conversely, you could schedule them at the end of the day and be headed home early.

You could do whatever you wanted with your Optas. There were no metal detectors and no hall monitors. Students could wander on and off campus at will, or just stroll the hallways leisurely. The result was hallways that were always teeming with students, as everybody kept a different schedule. Some of the seniors only had a couple of official classes per day. Presiding over this controlled chaos was Mr. Bruckner, a principal rumored to have such a keen photographic memory that he knew every single student's first and last name on sight. The place seemed like heaven to me—a level of responsibility almost impossible to believe.

This dramatic change in my life coincided with a major change in my mom's also. This was right around when she bought her co-op apartment on Cortelyou Road. While owning a home in most parts of the country is a given, it has always been a rarity in New York. As big a deal as it is for an upper middle-class family, it's an even bigger deal for a single mother working as a nurse. People in New York rent their apartments for decades.

People die paying rent and bugging the superintendent to fix broken heaters or leaky sinks. My mom's place was a big deal.

Mom had even changed nursing homes, a sign to her that she was moving up. To me, all of those places were depressing. Back in junior high I'd considered doing some volunteer work at her job, but one visit was enough to turn me off of it forever. As soon as you walked in the door, you could hear the moans of old people. I always found it interesting that the entire nursing staff was black (mostly West Indian), while almost all of the patients were white. These were real WASPs, the white people missing from our daily lives, holed up in Manhattan, where we rarely ventured. I saw the nursing home as the place where those people dumped their families. Nursing homes were where old white people came to die, and it was a terrible death. Mom warned me on numerous occasions, "you better *never* put me in one of these places."

Mike was going to Murrow too. It was nice to have one of my close friends making the jump to high school with me. Henry wasn't, but I was convinced he would when he finally made his high school decision. At Stranahan, students had the option of remaining for their eighth-grade year before moving on to high school, and Henry was one of those who stayed behind. Every time we got together, which was fairly often, I'd be certain to remind him just how great a place Murrow was. I'd tell him about the fine girls, the freedom to roam, and his eyes would light up.

Getting to school was also now much easier. It was a straight shot down Coney Island Avenue on the B68 bus. If the bus was too crowded, I could simply walk the distance in about twenty minutes. Murrow had its own conflicts, but they paled in comparison to Stranahan's. Most of the drama came from William E. Grady High, a vocational-technical ("Vo-tech") school that was dealing with metal detectors and all of the other issues that were forgotten by us after the first week. The Grady kids didn't like us. Once again, we weren't sure of the reason but guessed it had something to do with the fact that Grady was an all-boys school, and Murrow was overrun with gorgeous females. Nonetheless, when Grady kids passed us in their bus on Coney Island Avenue, they'd always curse at us or spit out of the windows in our direction. Rather than feel threatened, we found it rather amusing.

It wasn't like Murrow kids were exactly pushovers. While the school had an open door policy, "visitors" from rival schools couldn't just come strolling through the front door to start trouble at their leisure. Murrow's own little homegrown gang, the Po-Peo Posse, turned the back entrance into their makeshift headquarters, and could handle themselves against the roughest kids from any school in Brooklyn. It turns out that having the knucklehead contingent was kind of handy.

And did I mention the girls? They were plentiful, and they were so beautiful. While I still hadn't managed to get laid by this time, I was fairly confident that the moment was coming soon. Debbie was the object of my attraction, and it turns out that she lived in my apartment building. She hung out with another girl, Donna, who lived a few blocks away. Jerry and David, the other two guys who, together with Mike and me, formed a B68 riding foursome, had more courage when it came to flirting with and harassing the girls, but I was just pleased to see her every day in the building after school. I knew I'd eventually get my chance. How could I not? She lived in my apartment building, and we had to walk the two blocks from the bus stop to our building alone five days a week.

The old hierarchy was thrown out of wack at Murrow. There wasn't the same caste system that followed us around at Stranahan. It wasn't the jump or be jumped sets. Kids had a lot more foresight now. College recruiters were stopping by weekly from the Ivy Leagues, and the students who populated the theater and journalism programs were the fast-track types who dreamt of catching up to Murrow's most famous alumna, Marisa Tomei. Marisa was a recent graduate who'd landed a role on *The Cosby Show*'s college spin-off, *A Different World*. If there were any social classes at Murrow, it was those who were tough but smart, and those who were quirky and unusual.

I considered myself a smart kid, but I had no interest in being affiliated with the quirky kids. I didn't like Lenny Kravitz. I liked Eric B. & Rakim. The hardcore kids were the Jamaicans. These were kids who wore Clarks shoes instead of sneakers, and nice dress slacks instead of jeans. It was a uniform I'd already adopted thanks to my sister Stephany's relationship with Patrick, a Jamaican guy whose style I tried my best to emulate. These guys walked softly but carried huge sticks. They were gregarious, getting along equally well with white and black kids. One in my class, Jason, was particularly cool. So cool in fact that I decided to bring Mom's silver .25 pistol to school to show him. It wasn't loaded, of course. Bringing a loaded gun to school would be stupid. But he didn't know that. I flashed him the gun on the staircase. He gave an affirming smirk, then asked where I got it.

From home. This gun is mine.

He nodded in approval, and I tried my best to hold in the joy. Yes, I am moving up the food chain. I won't be getting bum-rushed anytime soon. I don't think there's any way things could get better. I wonder what Henry's up to this week?

• • •

The New York Times
APRIL 15, 1988, FRIDAY, LATE CITY FINAL EDITION
BOY, 14, SHOT TO DEATH; FRIENDS QUESTIONED

A 14-year-old Brooklyn boy died of a gunshot wound in the living room of a friend's apartment yesterday, the police said.

The shooting occurred in a second-floor apartment at 800 Cortelyou Road in the Brownsville section, according to Sgt. Raymond O'Donnell, a police spokesman.

Two other 14-year-old boys who were in the apartment at the time of the shooting around 6 PM. were being questioned by the police. The dead youth, who was shot in the head, was NAME DELETED of STREET ADDRESS DELETED Wyckoff Street, Brownsville. The names of the two other youths were withheld because of their age.

Sergeant O'Donnell said an initial investigation by the police indicated that the three boys were "handling the gun when it discharged."[*]

• • •

The telephone is ringing, but I'm hoping no one answers. I
don't know what to say, but I know I've been in this vacuum
long enough. A click, then an answer.

"Hello?"

Mike. It's me, Kemp.

"Holy shit, Kemp! Are you all right? Where are you?"

I'm back home.

"Oh," he said, followed by an uncomfortable silence as he
took in what that meant. I was back where it happened. Initially, I went to stay at my aunt's apartment in Coney Island for
a few days. Then I had to return home to my apartment, and the
dread was indescribable. Despite Mom's assurances that my
room looked fine, part of me was certain that Henry's body
would still be there, sprawled out on the floor.

Of course that wasn't the case, but it might as well have been
as I sifted through the belongings of his we had to gather to
return to his family. His long black trench coat. His backpack.
I opened it and flipped through his papers, a succession of
quizzes and exams. Each one had a score no lower than the
high nineties, and most had scores of one hundred, complete
with the happy face drawn into each of the zeroes.

I was pretty anxious to call Mike at first. He was a good
friend to both Henry and me, and I had to make certain
everyone at our old school knew what had happened, that it
had been a terrible accident. It turns out the news had traveled
fast, and it had hit 142 like a meteor.

"Man, people have been wondering what happened to you.
Mark was wondering if you were in jail. They told me that back
at 142 that girl Jamie, she was crying in the halls. She said she
couldn't believe it was you."

I was growing more sullen by the second, and questioning why I even decided to make the call in the first place.

"Yeah, and Johnny said . . ." then Mike paused.

What? What did he say?

"Well, he said that you did it on purpose. That you never really liked Henry anyway."

What?

"He was trying to put together a group of guys at school to come and get you. Joe told him he wasn't going to jump to any conclusions until he heard the whole story from you. But Johnny said if he ever sees you again, he's going to kill you."

How did I not see this coming? When Pat died, part of the reason the driver of the car was on suicide watch was because every person who knew him wanted to have his head. And that was an auto accident. This was many more levels questionable in nature. Still, I thought these guys were my friends, too. I couldn't believe anyone would suspect me of wanting to hurt Henry when we were closer than brothers for so long. We'd spent every moment outside of class together that last year at Stranahan, and now we were still seeing each other on a regular basis despite the distance. Was that the behavior of two guys who didn't really care about one another? It didn't make sense.

"Kemp?"

I was still silent, leaving Mike to hang on the other line.

"*I* know it was an accident."

That was the best thing I'd heard all day.

Henry's wake came too soon. I could not fathom Henry's family wanting me to attend, but my mother insisted we go. When I arrived at the funeral home, there was a large crowd gathered around the coffin. I assumed most of them were family members, although several of Henry's and my mutual friends were there. I first saw Mack, the person who'd originally introduced us. He was sitting in a small vestibule, crying. He looked up at me, smiled and waved.

I made my way over to the coffin to see Henry. He'd been made up well, in a nice suit. The entry wound was barely visible underneath the makeup. But the coffin made him look so *small*. I just stared at him, not knowing what to say, as our friend Jared placed a small cross on his lapel.

"I just want to see him!" a woman's voice blared out. I didn't know whether or not she was talking about Henry, lying there in the coffin, or me, his killer standing over him, tears dropping onto his blazer. I just closed my eyes and tried to shut out all of the noise. I knew every eye was trained on me, and all I could do was weep and continue wishing I were someplace else. I would not attend the funeral.

The Brooklyn courthouse where my case was heard was overcrowded. People lined up against the walls like they were in the unemployment line—only this was a line to see a judge for everything from child support to assault to (in my case) manslaughter. I felt uncomfortable in my suit, when most of the people in the room looked like they'd just rolled out of bed.

There were other teenagers in the courthouse, too. Lots of them. When Mom got up and left the room to find a vending machine, I turned to notice the kid sitting next to me staring right in my face. He was wearing a ratty t-shirt and picking his flattop.

"What are *you* doing here?"

He was an older kid, about seventeen years old. He was strangely by himself. No parent or friend in sight. I swallowed, breathed deeply and answered.

I shot somebody by mistake.

Suddenly the look of wariness left his face. He introduced himself: the police had stopped him and his friends in their car, and found a gun in the glove compartment. It wasn't his, he said, but his friend's. They were all Decepts.

I couldn't believe it. I'd heard about these guys. Among New York City teens, the Brooklyn Decepticons had become mythical in stature. Rumor had it that the Decepticons started back in 1986 when a handful of kids at Brooklyn Tech, one of the best schools in the city, banded together so they'd no longer get jumped and terrorized by other kids. It was like our idea for the K.A.H.T. Corps., but theirs actually caught on. The Decepts grew to include teenagers from all over Brooklyn and Manhattan. By now, people estimated they numbered more than five thousand members. They also morphed into a gang known for terrorizing kids in and around schools all over the city. Kings Plaza Mall, a popular hangout in Mill Basin, became off-limits to many of us because of its popularity among Decepticons, who liked to jump people waiting for the bus.

In reality, the Decepticon legend was probably overplayed, and I'd begun to doubt their existence. After all, I'd never encountered a single Decept before. Now I was sitting next to one and having a conversation. I wished that I wasn't. He was a nice enough guy, but his stories left me both frightened and appalled. He'd been living a life of stabbings and shootings, fighting and running. I did not want to be this guy. I didn't want to be anywhere near him.

Going back to school a few weeks later was tough. Initially, I'd begged my mother not to make me set foot in my old school again. I couldn't bear to face a single person I'd known. I was hoping at least to remain home for the remainder of the school year. No such luck. Less than two weeks after Henry died, I was once again walking the halls of Murrow, in a virtual trance. Mike was there with me, of course, being as supportive as he possibly could, but I was still paranoid. Whenever I got to a point where I began to feel comfortable, someone would hit me with a reminder. Once, Jerry and David joked on the bus ride home that shooting someone was my ploy to get on television. I didn't find it at all funny, but felt compelled to smile, as the kids on the bus cracked themselves up.

Jessica's reminders were much more affecting. She had attended Stranahan with us, and was now at Murrow. Before the Shooting, she always greeted Mike and me in the halls, and would occasionally strike up a chat. Now, she stopped speaking to me completely. Matt and I would still cross her path in the halls, and she would make every effort to greet him, then simply toss a cold stare in my direction, as though to say "shame on you" over and over again. I'd never seen her raise her voice to anyone, and I never felt threatened by her. But her eyes delivered a punishment with which neither fist nor shout could compare. I probably should have spoken to her about the incident, since it seemed to have affected her more than others. But I didn't, and I would never see her again after leaving high school.

The court-appointed counseling sessions were inconsequential at best. The social worker, Keith, was an astute, articulate man whose daughter attended Rutgers (he was very proud of that fact). I admire him now for committing so much of his personal life to helping troubled youngsters. Still, at the time, no matter how genuine his concern, he was ill equipped to handle a situation that didn't merit direct intervention. I suppose he'd been trained only to be the voice of reason, the positive influence necessary to sway troubled boys away from lives as drug dealers, robbers, and worse. He thought I didn't fit into the group. "You really don't belong here," he'd say on more than one occasion. "You're a good student. You *know* you made a mistake, and I don't think you'll make another one like that again."

Still, he encouraged my attendance at several group sessions, which to me were more like anthropological studies than forums for growth. Most of the kids in the group had obvious delinquency issues. I got to meet a few more elusive Decepticons. The sessions were similar to what one would expect when a kindergarten teacher tries to control a class full of small children. During one session, a television blared what looked like a homemade video of Public Enemy's "Bring the Noise," all while the rowdy boys shouted and swore at one another. Keith would lecture them (I say *them* because I sat silently throughout each session and simply listened, never interacting with any of the other boys), and they would brush off his comments like gnats on a summer day.

One kid nearly got into a fistfight with another. When Keith intervened and asked the aggressor what the problem was, his reply was curt. "He's fuckin' up my concentration while I'm tryin' to write my rhymes." I glanced at the crumpled piece of paper and the rap lyrics taking shape on the page, noting the misspelled words and weak composition. A career in music seemed like quite a stretch for this kid. I continued to sit there, silent. I had to get out of there.

The private sessions with Keith didn't fare much better. It wasn't that we didn't talk; Keith was as engaging as a counselor could be. It just seemed he was trained only to convince those who'd sinned that their wrongdoings had ramifications. *This system didn't have any contingency for someone who already displayed remorse.* It was just set up to help young offenders discover theirs. So we both went through the motions. The counseling ended within a year, and I was given my "not a sociopath" certification.

• • •

Disassociative amnesia is an amazing thing. I never thought that the human mind was capable of pushing a traumatic event so deep down into one's psyche that it begins to feel as though it never happened. The tragedy of Henry's death was driving me to become a success and to do him proud: up to that point I'd wanted to become a firefighter, but now that profession seemed too *small* to do Henry justice. I'd been given a second chance and felt an almost fanatic compulsion to achieve something big with my life. I needed to devote myself to becoming a success in something that I would be recognized for.

Nonetheless, the only way it was possible for me to function was to put Henry completely out of my mind. I knew I'd never make another mistake like that for as long as I lived, but I didn't need to replay his gruesome death over and over again in my head until it drove me to insanity.

It wasn't easy at first. Mom tried her best to help when she moved us from New York to Newport News, a small city in the Hampton Roads section of Virginia. But by that time, late in 1989, I no longer wanted to leave Brooklyn. I wanted to stay with my remaining faithful friends, Mike, Mack, Jerry, and David. My longtime crush, Debbie, and I had become friendly, and we walked each other home from school daily. There was a chance she and I were developing some kind of relationship, at least in my own diluted mind. I'd even become accustomed to Jessica's evil glares in the Murrow halls.

How was I able to cope so well, so quickly? Perhaps because the challenges of the day paled in comparison to the challenges of the night, when I had to sleep on the same bed that Henry had been sitting on when the bullet exploded in his jaw. The spots of blood remaining on the wall made my heart race so much, that after a while, it didn't race at all.

I didn't cope with the move to Virginia nearly as well. This was a place where there were no magnet programs. In fact, there wasn't much of anything. Gone were the multiracial groups of friends and the vibrant city life. In this part of Virginia, the world was divided into black and white. No Jamaicans. No Puerto Ricans. No Jews. No Italians. Just black kids and white kids. There wasn't the routine ethnic strife of Brooklyn, because there were no ethnic groups. The twin towers of the World Trade Center on the horizon were replaced by the towering cranes of Newport News Shipbuilding, one of the largest shipyards in the world.

Of course, the military was the other big presence in town, particularly among the black kids. In Hampton Roads, black kids play sports. That's just how it is. If you don't excel enough in football or basketball to get an athletic scholarship to college, then you join the military as soon as you graduate from high school. It's very cut and dry, and no one questions it. Perhaps that explains why so many pro athletes originate from this part of Virginia. From NBA player Allen Iverson (a product of Bethel High), to NFL Hall of Fame linebacker Lawrence Taylor (from nearby Williamsburg), the combines churned out athletes like California churns out surfers. Coming from an arts-oriented high school that didn't have competitive teams made me too unusual among my peers to go unnoticed. I didn't play basketball at all and my very limited abilities at football hadn't been on display since my Stranahan days, when we'd play lunchtime games on the playground in the shadow of the BQE. Even back then, throwing the football into triple coverage was usually a better option than tossing it in my direction, even if I was the only person open. My immediate search for the nearest well-stocked public library sent red flags up among all of the black kids in the cafeteria. I was as wary of them as they were of me.

Despite those reservations, being away from New York made it easier to suppress Henry's memory. And seeing the poverty and limited prospects of the kids in Hampton Roads reinforced my desire to make something of my life. I'd never smoked a cigarette or drunk a single beer before Henry died, and now I was adamantly opposed to doing anything that could be even remotely construed as objectionable.

Sex, of course, was an exception. I finally got laid—although it wasn't quite what I expected. After trying in vain to convince numerous girls to take the leap with me, the moment finally came with little fanfare. A girl named Erica I met during a summer job asked me if she could come over to my place for lunch. I told her sure. Mom wasn't around, so we started making out. No sweat, I'd done this before with plenty of girls. When Erica took off her clothes, I was thrown for a loop. Not knowing what to do next, I climbed on top of her, fumbling around trying to locate her vagina with my hard penis. No such luck. I was about to give up when she grabbed it, placed it inside of her, and began the stroking motion that ensured I lasted all of five seconds. A world record, perhaps, but another hurdle cleared.

As for sports, I had no interest in developing skill in basketball or football. I did, however, find much solace in full-contact sports. Punching and kicking a heavy bag was a great way to dull any emotional pain built up inside. My greatest therapy was Tae Kwon Do. I became the only member of an area sparring team who was under eighteen (I was sixteen), because the older boys loved my tenacity. I couldn't kick as high or punch as hard as some of the black belts, but I'd take punishment and keep on coming, losing myself in the flurry of punches and kicks. That tenacity drove me to several city martial arts championships. In fact, anger was now the driving force behind everything I did. Anger at being so different. Anger at being in Virginia instead of New York. And anger at feeling so alone. While Tae Kwon Do was my purest, most base outlet for this rage, it wasn't the only one. Anger drove me to perform well on exams in my advanced placement classes, simply to spite the teachers I felt did not want me there. Anger drove me to read every book I could get my hands on, because my smug white classmates all thought they were smarter than me by default. By my senior year in high school, I'd become emotionally distant from my family—even more so than your typical teenager—spending long hours alone in my room, reading and dreaming about where I'd go in the world. But I was no longer intimidated by anyone. In fact, it was just the opposite. I was always anxious for a fight. And why wouldn't I be? I could do knuckle push-ups on cinder blocks without even flinching.

Despite the protests of several teachers, who thought a life in the military would be perfect for me, I decided to go to college. The Ivy Leagues were no longer of any interest to me. I'd had enough of trying to fit into anyone else's groups. I chose Howard University, a predominantly black college in Washington, D.C., both because I hoped to be surrounded by like-minded peers and because my inner Herb had been longing to visit the famous Smithsonian Institution since I was a child. Howard was where my writing career began, both as a reporter for my school newspaper and as a fiction writer for a series of self-published underground comic books. In less than ten years, I'd go from a scared, self-obsessed child trying to survive on the streets, to a headstrong professional journalist with a wife and child. In 1998 I made my triumphant return to New York City, pregnant wife in tow. I'd done well for myself. I'd nabbed the first editorial internship at *Smithsonian Magazine* shortly after arriving at Howard. I'd done public relations for the world-famous Guthrie Theater in Minneapolis. I'd started writing regularly for publications ranging from alternative weekly newspapers to large national magazines. But now it was time to go home. I'd been working hard, and it was time to reap the benefits in the place that raised me, even though I'd managed not to acknowledge the reason I was trying so hard in the first place.

I spoke to Henry's older brother James for the last time during my freshman year at Howard. It was a monumental event for me, making that call, since some part of me expected Henry's family to have changed their minds about their forgiveness. Maybe they just woke up one morning and thought "screw this, that little bastard owes!" Or maybe the pain became overwhelming, and their love was replaced with anger, much like the anger that was driving me to outdo my peers in everything I attempted.

I called James from my dorm room, and we chatted for fifteen minutes or so. He seemed to be having a good life, and he inquired with general interest about what I was doing. He was about to head into the police force. I was proud to inform him that I was a great student, and was well on my way to a career as a writer. I would call him again a few years later, but a woman answered the telephone and curtly said, "he doesn't live here anymore." Perhaps his marriage had hit a major hurdle? I'd never know, and I didn't want to call and bother the angry woman again.

•   •   •

"Kemp, come up here!"

The urgency in my wife Nicole's voice was evident. My eighteen-month-old daughter, Mackenzie, had fallen asleep in her arms not twenty minutes ago, when she took her upstairs and placed her in her crib. She'd had a nagging fever, but nothing either of us were concerned about, and we were giving her a regular dose of children's Tylenol. After laying her down, Nicole returned to the living room and we were chatting for several minutes. Since returning to the city, my services as a writer had become quite in demand, and it seemed like I was always juggling an endless number of writing deadlines. By the time my daughter was born in August 1998, I had exceeded even my own personal expectations. We'd even managed to move from our one-bedroom apartment in Woodside to a nice duplex rental in Jamaica Estates. We could hear Mackenzie coughing a little, so Nicole decided to head upstairs to check on her.

"Kemp, get up here quick!"

I ran up the stairs—and was greeted by my worst nightmare. Nicole held our baby daughter, who stared up at me in a daze, covered in her own vomit.

We sped to the hospital. My wife gently rocked the baby and whispered to her, "mommy and daddy love you." The words put me into a trance. I was experiencing a familiar rush that I'd long since forgotten.

How could I be going through this again? What mistake did I make this time?

By the time we reached the emergency room, the baby's body had begun to convulse. *The convulsions again.* The memories came back to me in a rush. The helplessness. The panic. The things I hadn't felt since the Shooting, ten years before. Was this to be my punishment, to feel how Henry's parents must have felt when they lost him?

I cried all night as the doctors fought for my daughter's life.

• • •

Mackenzie made it. As it turned out, the nagging fever she'd been experiencing had triggered febrile seizures. She'd vomited when the seizures began, then inhaled a large amount of the vomit, clogging her lungs. We were given a miracle that day, and she recovered fully. Still, the ordeal dredged up a wellspring of familiar emotions I hadn't anticipated.

I'd never had any nightmares about the Shooting. Maybe it was because it was so much on my thoughts during the day that at night my exhausted mind just drew a blank. After Mackenzie's brush with death, that all changed. I began having a strange dream in which I rose from my bed and turned to face Henry. He was there, sitting in my room, with the bullet hole still in his chin. I'd talk with him, the conversation initially limited to pleasantries. How are you? How are you doing? His blank stare betrayed no emotion, and eventually I began apologizing, asking him if he knew how sorry I was. Asking him if he knew that I'd have never shot him on purpose. He stares blankly for several more seconds, then tries to respond. But when he opens his mouth, no sounds come out, as though the wound is still preventing him from speaking. After nearly screaming at him in hopes of a response, I simply give up and begin to cry.

I'd wake up in tears, not the least bit frightened, but incredibly sad. I just wanted to have a conversation with him again. It made me wish I were Buddhist instead of Protestant—the idea of all souls melding into one nebulous form after death was a more comforting one than an afterlife where you meet those you knew when alive. Because when Henry and I meet again, what will the grown man have to say to his fourteen-year-old friend?

I can't help but feel this is some sort of sign, and I begin to recall several other signs I received before Mackenzie's sickness. Shortly after arriving back in New York, I found Henry on my mind when I realized I didn't have a single photograph of him. I was myself struggling to recall the details of his face. I remembered the features, yet couldn't put them all together into a cohesive image in my head.

Then, during a trip to Paris while working on an assignment, I brushed up against his spitting image. While strolling around Les Halles, fighting through the crowd near the Pompidou Centre, I saw Henry again. The boy was Arab instead of Puerto Rican, but they could have been twins. The image of Henry's face was burned back into my mind, but I didn't take it as anything more than a simple coincidence.

Now I knew that it meant something. When my daughter got sick, I suddenly felt like a marked man, singled out for my great misdeed. I had no desire to be left alone in a room with Mackenzie, even when she was laughing and wanting to play. I just knew that as soon as we were alone, something would go wrong. Something would happen, and I'd have another death on my hands.

• • •

It was a long and strange trip back to the city of my birth. And though I never would've admitted it before Mackenzie fell ill, I hadn't gotten very comfortable after that return to New York. While I'd left the city grudgingly, I'd become quite comfortable being away. There was something empowering about being "a

New Yorker living in fill-in-the-blank," which was how I
always described myself. While gingerly stepping into the
waters of Buckroe Beach in Hampton, Virginia, trying desperately to avoid the stings of jellyfish, I was a New Yorker living
in the sticks. When walking past the Nation of Islam mosque
in Washington, D.C., on my way to get a haircut at Shabazz bar-
bers, I was a New Yorker living in Chocolate City. While plug-
ging my car into a wall outlet to recharge the battery and while
scraping the ice from my windshield during a Minneapolis
winter, I was a New Yorker living in the Tundra.

Carrying the city with me to all of these places had in so
many ways romanticized it. Much like in those Renaissance
paintings, when the lower classes are portrayed as living a life
of plebian leisure, my life in New York had taken on an air of
nostalgia. That nostalgia only dissipated when it came time to
return, when there was a sudden reluctance to pick up the life
I'd left behind.

Of course, there were pragmatic reasons for not returning to
New York. The incredible cost of living. My wife's Midwestern
upbringing and hesitance to live in the cramped big city. My
reluctance to come full circle was simply a handy deal-sealer
to finalize the decision, no matter how many opportunities
arose. However, deep down inside I wanted to return. If I
didn't, I'd have never become a journalist. The unavoidable
truth is that journalism is a profession in which all roads eventually lead to New York. Of course, one could fashion a
respectable career working for a large publication in one of its
bureaus, but if you perform at a high level and with a skill that
garners respect from your peers, then the gods will eventually
call you home. Home to New York City.

I considered performing at a high level a given. I'd lucked out with two great mentors in college. The first, Ethelbert, was a prominent D.C. poet who helped temper and redirect at least some of my anger into projects such as internships and writing contests. The second, Janice, was my boss during my first Smithsonian internship, and she took it upon herself to help me locate other positions that would further my writing career. I'd also lucked out in having my first internship at a place populated by Art History and Philosophy graduates instead of J-School students. It's not like I went into college even knowing that I wanted to become a writer. Quite the opposite. I'd entered college unsure of what I wanted to do, and even more uncertain of whether or not I was capable of doing anything.

Virginia, while an escape from the oppression of the city, had been a major blow to my self-esteem. I'd already stood out among my new peers just by the way I dressed and my relative ignorance about things that were considered common in the south ("what do you mean you've never gone to a homecoming parade?"). Compounding that was the fact that I not only lacked a southern accent, but spoke with a diction so proper that the first response of most girls when I opened my mouth was "damn, you sound white!" My being a New Yorker was the icing on the cake. Unfortunately, New Yorkers were abundant seasonal visitors to the Hampton Roads area, and not just to visit the nearby Virginia Beach strip.

When driving south from New York, drivers pass through many states before entering Virginia. There's New Jersey, Delaware, Maryland, and (sometimes) Washington, D.C. However, Virginia is the first of a long strip of southern states where gun laws are shockingly lax. Virginia was the state that supplied

New York street thugs with their arsenals. There were gun stores everywhere, and picking up a firearm was fast and cheap. Dealers who brought the guns back to New York could turn around and sell them for several times what they paid. The profit margins would make a CEO envious.

Gun control has been an amusing topic to me ever since, because when you live in an environment where you see how easily such laws are circumvented, it makes the entire debate for or against gun control completely pointless. I decided back then, at that young age, that there either had to be one universal law regulating firearm ownership, or none at all. The guys I knew who wanted guns would get them regardless of the obstacles. If Virginia had stringent gun laws, they'd drive down to North Carolina to buy them. If North Carolina adopted legislation, they'd head down to Georgia. If there's one thing thugs don't mind doing, it's driving: I knew guys who'd drive to Idaho if there was a Wal-Mart sale on Beretta nine-millimeter pistols.

But Virginia was the first of the southern states, and as a result, much of the abundant New York element in the state was of the decidedly thug variety. And not just in a general, nebulous sense. One of my most notorious cousins, a petty criminal and thug who shared my last name, had already arrived on the scene a year earlier, and landed with quite a splash. I'd utter my name to kids in school, and they'd immediately respond, "are you related to . . . ?" When I'd nod, they'd shoot a sideways glance, as though they were trying to figure out how the two of us could possibly be related.

While I didn't fit the profile of the Brooklyn knucklehead, my ability to socialize equally well with honors students and hardcore felons put me in an unusual position. My hangout buddies after school were some of the hardest kids around. Kids like Keith, Darrell, and D.C. I didn't even realize these guys were the tough element at school, considering the hard edge that everyone in Brooklyn seemed to have. It only dawned on me after a number of events sent up red flags. When Keith called me from the city jail to chat, for example.

"What's up, Kemp?"

Hey Keith. What you doin?

"Man, I'm downtown in city jail."

What?

"Yeah, they locked me up for some bullshit."

(pause)

Are you all right? You want me to come down there or something?

"Oh, naw man. I'm cool. There's actually a few cats that I know in here too. I was just callin' to say what's up and talk. I'm boreder than a mutherfucker."

Even though I wasn't getting thrown in jail or getting into any trouble, I garnered a certain level of respect from my little crew. Everybody at school knew I was a full-time Tae Kwon Do combatant. Sure, I wouldn't touch a gun, but if it was any other kind of fight, they knew I'd put my foot in someone's ass, and fast. In fact, my temper got shorter and shorter with every passing week. When hanging out with my testosterone-driven sparring team, we'd wander area shopping malls looking for someone to pick a fight with. Unfortunately, the people we'd confront over little transgressions tended to back down. Eventually, we'd take to making homemade kung-fu movies with

Mom's camcorder. It gave us a good excuse to kick each other in the head outside of practice.

Even more sudden than my transformation into bitter teen pugilist was the change in the racial makeup of those I associated with. Soon after arriving in Virginia, almost all of my friends became black. Sure, I was once again one of only two black kids in all of the advanced placement courses, but unlike in Brooklyn, I wasn't fraternizing with my white classmates. It just didn't feel comfortable. They seemed to make huge assumptions about me that even the bigoted Italian kids back in the city never did. Assumptions about what I read, what I knew, where I grew up, and what music I liked.

Yeah, I loved hip hop, but that was never the only kind of music I listened to. In fact, some of my Depeche Mode and Thomas Dolby tapes were the most worn out in my collection. Did people honestly believe that the early practitioners of hip hop in New York only listened to rap music? News flash: *there was no rap music before them.* Impresarios like Russell Simmons probably spent as much time in their middle-class homes listening to the same music their white counterparts did: rock, funk, and disco. Yet it was easy for white kids in places like Virginia to simply assume that we exited the womb humming verses from "Rapper's Delight." I was often so insulted by my new classmates' assumptions that I'd play dumb just to toy with them. *Johnny Cash? Yeah, I know who he is. He was that old guy that got his ass kicked by an ostrich, right?*

The one exception to the rule was Philip, a half-Filipino, half-white kid who became the primary person I ran around with. Philip and I shared a love for reading and mischief. We'd head to Patrick Henry Mall on weekends to steal books from the bookstore. In one whirlwind summer we read *The Autobiography of Malcolm X*, the Malcolm X FBI Tapes, the Quran, Sun Tzu's *The Art of War*, Bruce Lee's *Tao of Jeet Kune Do*, the *Tao Teh Ching*, and *The Once and Future King*. In fact, I was reading more books now than I ever had back home. There was nothing else to do, since there wasn't exactly a line of girls at my front door waiting to have sex with me.

It's easy to critique children living in the city as having a predisposition for getting in trouble. A city like New York certainly has its own unique challenges for the young person growing up. However, Hampton Roads helped me realize that the obstacles we had to navigate on Brooklyn's streets also served as a distraction and often helped deter us from getting into trouble.

In Virginia, where the suburban lifestyle was the norm, there were no battery-chucking subway hooligans. No graffiti-marred public buildings. Things were quiet, everyone owned a home, and every home had several cars parked in the driveway. The result was a young population that was so bored with the sterile nature of their lives all they seemed to do was get into trouble.

A friend of mine said it best soon after I arrived: "Man, down here, the only thing to do is fuck and fight."

The fucking part was one thing I didn't mind, but it was still unsettling to come across so many pregnant freshmen at War-wick High. At Murrow in Brooklyn, I'd never known a single pregnant girl. If a girl did get knocked up, it was basically her ticket out of school. She'd be ostracized if she stayed. Things could not have been more different at Warwick. I counted several girls walking the halls at least seven months pregnant in my first week. Once the shock of their maternity wear wore off, I'd look around to see if anyone else noticed these mothers-in-waiting. There was never a response. It was as though they were all invisible.

The sex culture was so blasé that it made getting seriously involved with any girl a real chore. Guys back in Brooklyn would try to marry the first girl they slept with and kill one of their friends if they dared to date her, even if years had passed after the breakup. At Warwick, it was as though every guy in school had slept with every girl. Multiple times.

During one of my science classes, I talked to the little crew at my particular table about a girl I was considering asking to the prom. Our teacher had lost about eighty percent of his sight, so you could carry on outside of his direct line of vision and he'd never notice.

"If you do go out with her, make sure she sucks your dick, ok?"

What do you mean?

"I mean you should at least get your dick sucked for taking her anywhere. She sucked mine in the parking lot when I took her to see *Home Alone*."

Pretty soon, almost every girl at school seemed tainted. I couldn't say hello to Tammy without immediately envisioning her going down on my buddy in a parking lot. When Charmaine said she thought I was cute, all I could see was another friend of mine ejaculating on her face and walking out of the door. It was going to be a long, hard time down in Virginia for me.

Fortunately, the fighting came much easier thanks to my

circle of aggressive friends. Maybe it was the culture of football games and the Tae Kwon Do. Whatever it was, there always seemed to be plenty of good reasons to punch someone in the face. When Philip came to school one day with a bandage on his head and explained how he got jumped by some kids from another high school while visiting his girlfriend, I made it my civic duty to pull about ten people out of their classes. We drove across town to the offending kid's house, where Carl kicked down the front door while the frightened teen's mom called the police. After a few punches in the kid's face, we retreated to the corner and taunted him from a distance.

"Don't fuck with Philip!" Philip sheepishly proclaimed as he jumped into the backseat of my car.

I had left Brooklyn naïve about the world and oblivious to everything in my world, and transformed seemingly overnight into a militant townie.

Mom and me.

Dad and two of my older sisters, Sharon (on his head)
and Sheila.

(above) My sister Steph and me at Sheila's high school graduation in Coney Island, about 1980.

(opposite page) Me and Mr. T at Comicfest '94.

(top of opposite page) From left: Jerry, David, and Mike, my closest friends at Murrow High.

(bottom of opposite page) Me (left) and my friends in Virginia from the Tae Kwon Do team. Oh, and Philip (the white guy).

(right) Freshman year at Howard with friends.

(above) At the first convention for our new comic book company in 1993 (Washington, D.C.).

(opposite page) My daughter, Mackenzie, enjoying her first lemon ice with her mom in Corona, Queens (summer 2000).

(above) My car after the accident that pushed me over the edge in Chicago.

An excerpt from my first comic book, *Flatbush Native*, issued by Flatline
Comics. The superhero, Akil, has incredible powers but can only activate
them by first taking the life of another person—which gives him a cynical,

almost nihilistic viewpoint on life. I was invited on CNN's *Sonya Live* to talk about the effects of media violence on young people—but I never mentioned my own history with violence.

Part Three.

Historically Black Colleges and Universities have provided generations of students with access to highly supportive environments for learning. Their experience and expertise make them an invaluable resource to our nation during this period of significant change.

—Excerpt from a proclamation by President Bill Clinton
September 22, 1997

If you're black, in order to succeed in this world, you need to work ten times as hard as your white counterparts. You can't just be "average." That's a fact of life you learn to live with, and just one of the things I learned from going to Morehouse.

—Spike Lee, Morehouse alumnus
Minneapolis, MN
October 9, 1997

Not only do we manufacture revolutionaries here at Howard, but we manufacture Negroes. Don't leave here and just disappear

117.

*into the "Negro machine." I understand you need to do your
own thing, but your thing needs to be* our *thing.*

*—Amiri Baraka, Howard University alumnus, addressing a
group of students at Founder's Library
Howard University
October 14, 1997*

M y militant stance continued and festered in college.
Howard University, in Washington, D.C., was heaven for
me: it provided the like-minded peer group I'd always desired
but never really had growing up—aside from a handful of
friends at Murrow. Also, I'd held a deep-seated desire to visit
and work at the Smithsonian Institution, and I figured living in
D.C. would provide me with the opportunity to make that happen.

Howard, like all Historically Black Colleges and Universities (HBCUs), was an interesting place. The "typical" Howard
student was not an underprivileged city kid, but a middle- to
upper-middle-class product of the suburbs. It seemed that
most Howard students spent their developmental years
attending private schools, and when the time to select a college
came around, the choices included the usual selection of elite
institutions. The Cornells and Northwesterns of the world.
They chose Howard because of its promise of providing the one
thing their upbringing could not: other black people.

Even today, discussing Howard University and other HBCUs
with faculty members and students is sort of like talking to a
mother whose son is always in trouble. Her love is apparent, as
well as her criticism and anger over his actions. It's a family

thing, and outsiders usually have no business even asking questions about "what's going on" at black colleges.

What is it that makes attending an HBCU a better option than any other college? Why should a promising black student choose a school like Howard University over the promise (and clout) of Stanford? The answer is simple: The Black Experience.

The black experience is intangible, and it carries a different meaning depending on whom you pose the question to. For some, it means being in an environment that nurtures and promotes black thought. For many, it means nationalism and cultural empowerment: black folks being able to "do their own thing;" it's the proverbial finger in the face of whitey. For others, it means unwillingly getting to witness every problem endemic to the black community as it's carried over to the university level, from crime to the black "good old boy" network.

Most of the larger black colleges were created near the turn of the century as institutions to educate free blacks in a segregated America. America's earliest black scientists, doctors, lawyers, and entrepreneurs all received their education at institutions such as Howard, Morehouse, Spelman, Tuskegee, Lincoln, Hampton, and the many other black colleges spread across the American South. In 1947, when Jackie Robinson hit his first home run as a member of the Brooklyn Dodgers, these schools were the thriving centers of African American thought and politics. Future black author Langston Hughes was teaching writing classes at Atlanta University Center, renown historian John Hope Franklin was still teaching at Howard University and diligent students such as the future civil rights activist Medgar Evers were hitting the books at smaller black schools like Alcorn A&M College. By the time I'd arrived on Howard's campus, HBCUs could still boast having over sixty-five percent of the practicing black physicians in the United States as graduates, as well as fifty percent of black engineers, fifty percent of black business executives, thirty-five percent of black lawyers, and eighty percent of black judges.

Ironically enough, with Jackie Robinson's opening of the opportunity floodgates for black athletes, the Negro Leagues were quickly drained of talent, fans, and money by the major leagues, and they abruptly vanished. The three thousand institutions of higher education followed the lead of professional sports, and with the 1954 Supreme Court decision of *Brown v. Board of Education*, the nation saw the legal desegregation of all institutions of higher education. In the decades that followed, promising black students, athletes, and professors began an exodus to larger, better funded, predominantly white institutions, leaving the black schools strapped for students, scholars, and cash. Many of the smaller black schools, such as Central State University and Texas Southern University, have teetered on the verge of bankruptcy for years, and some of the larger ones, such as Howard, were suffering from deteriorating infrastructure and facilities by the time I arrived.

Of course, not all black colleges have the same problems, and not all of these problems are even unique to black institutions. While schools like Howard University and Morehouse have always had to adapt to their locations in decaying inner-city neighborhoods, the same problem besets large predominantly white institutions, such as the University of Chicago or Tulane, or Yale, to name a few. (And for every Morehouse or Howard addressing issues of crime and environment, there are rural black colleges, such as Hampton University, that boast the manicured campuses one expects in the Ivy Leagues.) Another shared trait is the bloated administrative bureaucracy and "good old boy networks" of white institutions (particularly state operated ones). However, despite these similarities, there is one unifying problem at almost every black college or university, and it's the one problem that most large white schools never have to worry about: money. Or more precisely, a lack of it.

Financial resources are what enable schools like the University of Chicago to maintain a staff of professors including a dozen Nobel Prize winners. It's money that attracts prospective students of all colors to large universities with the promise of state-of-the-art research facilities. It's money that keeps the lights on and the campuses connected to the outside world. And it's money that has caused many black colleges to descend to a kind of "second tier" status in the eyes of many students and teachers.

Searching for the nation's most comprehensive and respected African American studies department? Look to Harvard. How about the Givens Collection, which contains over six thousand rare volumes of black literature? Head to the University of Minnesota. Poet Laureate and Author Maya Angelou? She's a Wake Forest University professor. Scholar and presidential advisor John Hope Franklin? Try Duke University. Nobel Prize winning author Toni Morrison? Bounce to Princeton University. And let's not even talk about the black-dominated collegiate sports of basketball and football, which rake in millions in television deals for white institutions, while most black colleges waddle around in obscurity in unknown divisions.

Nowhere were all of the financial ordeals facing black colleges more evident than at Howard. Fiscal crises had been the norm at "The Mecca" for years, and by the early nineties many of the campus facilities had deteriorated to near third world status. The library, hailed as a treasure trove of black history and culture, utilized an antiquated (and usually inoperable) computer system that made it nearly impossible for students to find the books of their choice. Far-flung dormitories such as Sutton Hall were islands in the middle of D.C.'s seediest neighborhoods, and everything from student prostitution rings to turf wars between students and local drug dealers graced the pages of the student newspaper, *The Hilltop*, so frequently that the local media didn't even bother covering these crimes. On campus, the facilities didn't fare much better, as dorms like Drew Hall featured rooms with bullet-hole-riddled windows, and garbage cans outside the School of Business were often overrun by hordes of gigantic sewer rats. I considered life in my freshman dormitory quite similar to living in a housing project.

With this new city and new chapter in my life came yet another new crew of friends. Only this time, we weren't forced upon each other by circumstance. We had all chosen to be here at Howard. Most of what would later become known as "Diss Tribe" met in the basement of Howard University's Armour J. Blackburn Center, either in the cafeteria or the adjacent "Punch-Out," a retro seventies dining hall that is the preferred on-campus hangout of most upperclassmen.

Nathan was a D.C. native, and one of the first people I met at Howard. I'd actually met him the summer before school began, when I drove up from Virginia for a special weekend preorientation program. Nathan was a cool guy who sported circular rimmed glasses and tiny dreadlocks. His family was from New Orleans, and his parents had met when they were both attending Xavier, a black college in the city.

Sean was also at preorientation weekend, but he wasn't a D.C. kid. He hailed from Cambridge, Massachusetts. His family was West Indian, but Sean looked more like an East Indian kid than anything else. His defining feature was the tail he kept cut into the back of his head.

I met Ornette during the first week of classes. Sean introduced the two of us as we were walking to the Blackburn Center. Ornette, or "O," was from nearby Baltimore. He was studying graphic design in Howard's Fine Arts school.

Kebbi was O's roommate in Drew Hall. He was also a fine arts student, but his focus was music—specifically, the saxophone. A native of Atlanta, Kebbi's father had also been a jazz musician, which caused his family to have some reservations about his pursuing music in college.

Will was a classmate of O's in several fine arts courses. Also a graphic design major, Will hailed from Richmond. His older sister was a Howard upperclassman. While technically studying graphic design, Will's real love was illustration.

Doug was a native of Altadena, California. He was also staying in Drew Hall, and hadn't decided on his major when we first met. He was very interested in writing, though.

Adilson, or Dil, was from Boston. Unlike Sean, he wasn't West Indian. He was Cape Verdean. Cape Verde is a small country off the western coast of Africa. Huge numbers of Cape Verdeans had relocated to the Boston area for years. Being Cape Verdean meant Dil spoke fluent Portuguese. He also had two cousins attending Howard, Al and Cass.

Dave was the only other kid from New York who I became close to at Howard. He was from Brooklyn, too, and was Jamaican, but didn't have an accent. We met in one of my first classes, Humanities, and got along immediately. He didn't have the same interest in reading Chinua Achebe's *Things Fall Apart* or the mythical African tale of Sundiata that I did, but it was his honest apathy that was endearing. Everyone else at Howard seemed caught up in a personal quest for Afrocentrism, and Dave was much more concerned about simply passing his next exam than reaffirming his blackness. It seemed like we were among the only New York kids there who actually hailed from one of the five boroughs. Most kids who claimed to be from New York were either from Long Island or upstate.

Howard in many ways mirrored Brooklyn. Once again, it was a chore simply navigating your way to an education. The hostility directed at Howard students from the people in the surrounding neighborhood was palpable. They saw us as uppity. In fact, many Howard students *were* uppity—still, no one deserved the treatment the student body was prone to receive from the neighborhood. Robberies were a routine occurrence, and walking to campus from the nearest subway station at night was a true test of nerves. Out of our little crew of friends, O, Will, Nathan, Sean, and Kebbi were all mugged at least once.

One of the first endeavors I undertook after arriving on

campus was starting a fledgling comic book company with some of my classmates. It made perfect sense, considering our divergent interests and studies. Will loved comic illustration, but had no story ideas to illustrate. O's more serious graphic skills leant themselves perfectly to comic book design and layout, as well as inking, coloring, and lettering. I'd discovered somewhere between junior high and college that I had a knack at writing. During the first week of classes at Howard, when we were given a writing aptitude test, my English teacher, Ms. Banks, was so impressed by my writing that I was exempted from taking any freshman writing courses. It was a confidence and ego boost that helped me fall in love with the medium. However, my drawing skills weren't quite up to scratch— during drafting class in elementary school, I couldn't draw a straight line even with the assistance of a T-square, which undoubtedly perplexed my teacher.

All three of us were infatuated with comic books, and had been for years. I don't know when and where O's and Will's love affair with them began, but mine started when I was in sixth grade and purchased my first issue of *The Uncanny X-Men* from Brain Damage Comics. The X-Men were unlike the sterile superheroes of the D.C. Comics universe. Heroes like Superman and Wonder Woman, with their patriotic tights, seemed more like recruitment tools for the U.S. Army than living, breathing people. The X-Men, on the other hand, had depth. They were three-dimensional characters, each with his or her own shortcomings. My favorite—as well as the favorite of millions of other adolescents—had always been the adamantium-clawed Wolverine.

The excitement I first felt when I read an issue of an X-Men comic was a feeling that wouldn't be duplicated until my teens (when I finally had my first fumbling sexual encounter). It was that lack of excitement in comics we were lamenting one day in my dorm room when the idea of starting our own comic company started. O and Will were more than willing to draw, but they were at a loss for any original ideas for superheroes. No problem, I told them: I had an idea for a unique superhero no one had ever seen before.

We named the company Flatline Comics for no reason other than the fact that it sounded cool. However, the content of our stories ended up meriting the name. They were gritty, stark tales, and I was responsible for writing most of them along with Doug. My first original story was called *Flatbush Native*. It was about a more realistic super being who had great powers. He could fire bolts of energy and had superhuman strength. He could project the energy behind him to fly for short distances. He could even melt bullets fired at him before they got close enough to do any damage.

However, in order to activate these incredible powers, he first had to take the life of another person by draining that person's life essence. I figured adding that caveat to his powers would make him more hesitant to use them, and my protagonist, Akil, only activated his powers to get himself out of a tight spot. Another downside to his abilities was that, once activated, Akil had to discharge all of his energy within a few minutes or it would eat away at *his* body and kill him. Thus, activating his powers meant taking a human life and, once activated, those powers could never be used in moderation. I wanted him to represent the nihilistic attitude of Brooklyn that I hadn't noticed until I left.

In the opening scene of the first issue, Akil awakens one night to a woman being assaulted and raped in the alley outside his window. He looks down at her and considers helping, then decides to go back to sleep. His rationale? *She should have known better than to be out at this time of night anyway.*

Though I never said it to my partners, the rape scene in the first issue represented the afternoon of Henry's death, when I knocked on my neighbor's door and he wouldn't come out to help. Later on, after the police arrived, I remembered his smile, and his know-it-all attitude, and I became enraged. Of course, if he had decided to help, he wouldn't have been able to save Henry. Still, it was nice having someone else other than myself to pin blame on. Similar things occurred on a regular basis in Brooklyn back then. I could recall lazy afternoons hanging out my window and watching kids strip cars down like a NASCAR pit team, all while pedestrians and traffic passed by, unconcerned. My comic book was meant to be a scathing indictment of that culture of noninvolvement.

The D.C. press found out about our comics and made other observations. They thought our books symbolized some kind of new nihilism among young people. Why were these young men, these Flatliners, so angry at the world? As the company's editor-in-chief, I had most of the face time on television. I went on CNN's *Sonya Live*, where I participated in a roundtable discussion on the influence of media violence on today's youth. Also on the panel were gun advocate and rocker Ted Nugent, a shrink, and some kid from Hunter College High in New York who said he was addicted to playing the video game *Mortal*

Kombat. I couldn't mention my personal experiences when discussing the reasons for my grim tales. I just explained that I didn't think they were that grim anyway. They just reflected my reality. The world was a cold, cruel place. Nugent then started rambling about how young punks should be drawn and quartered.

The comic business was going well, but not well enough. It became difficult for us to continue putting out the issues on a regular basis while still going to class. In addition to writing, penciling, inking, and lettering the books, we had to get the covers colored by a digital separation company. Then we had to get the books printed. For the first two issues we used a small D.C. area printer, but as our print runs increased to more than five thousand copies per issue, we had to find cheaper alternatives, so we began having them done by Quebecor printing in Montreal, Canada. Distribution was sketchy at first. Though first Capital City and eventually Diamond Comics Distribution circulated our books to comic book stores around the country, in those initial stages we had to distribute by hand at comic book conventions. Weekends consisted of trips to cities like Philadelphia, New York, and Atlanta to peddle our wares. Usually we drove. Sometimes we took the bus. And the trips were very difficult on all of us physically and emotionally. During Comicfest '94 in Philadelphia, the biggest comic book convention in the country that year, we actually procured an exhibitor booth in the main hall. During the day, we signed comics and mingled with fans. We even got to enjoy the convention a little ourselves. I got to take a photo with Mr. T, the only photo with a celebrity I've ever taken, even though I've probably interviewed more than a hundred. I'd loved Mr. T since watching him in *The A-Team,* and found myself star-struck. I've interviewed and written stories about people much more famous, but I've never been as thrilled to meet anyone as I was to meet Mr. T that day.

The fun ended at night though. It turns out there was a Harley Davidson convention in Philadelphia the same week, so when we decided to leave our hotel after a minor dispute with a hotel worker, we had no idea we'd be met with NO VACANCY signs everywhere in the city. After we were finally kicked out of a hospital emergency room, we spent the next several nights sleeping on the streets. We took turns holding onto our sales stash from the convention, which ballooned to nearly two thousand dollars in comic book sales, and prayed we didn't get held up.

While sitting on the steps outside of a hotel near the convention center, Todd McFarlane, then the writer of the popular comic book *Spawn,* saw us and invited a couple of us up to his hotel room. He was still wearing women's stockings as part of a gag he'd done during a presentation earlier that day. He and his roommate, Erik Larsen (writer and artist of another popular comic, *Savage Dragon*), looked over our comics and commended us on our work. It was a nice ego boost that made the trip feel worthwhile. Then McFarlane told us he had to get ready for a party. He and Larsen signed copies of every comic we had in our possession, then sent us on our way. Once we were booted back onto the streets, reality negated any positive reinforcement that we'd received up in the room, and we took refuge near the entrance to the convention center. We slept in shifts.

Within a year, juggling class and company duties was nearly

impossible. We brought in more classmates to help, but instead of relieving the workload, it just got worse. By the end of the second year, our fledgling company had gone out of business, but it had also given me an entry into the world of writing. My comic book writing and management experience were the points on my young resume, along with my writing for *The Hilltop*, that got me through the door for my first editorial internships. I was back on the path to success, despite my detour in the wilds of Virginia.

Unfortunately, a snafu in Howard University's administration department resulted in my financial aid paperwork not being properly filed one semester, and several classes I had been taking were tossed out due to my lack of payment. I was so disgusted by the situation that I decided to leave the university. I didn't have time for the nonsense of an inept administration department anyway. Success awaited me.

• • •

My move to Minnesota was a calculated one. With my lack of serious editorial experience, I knew the going would be tough financially in New York. If I were alone, roughing it would have been fine, but by now I considered myself engaged to my girlfriend Nicole, and I knew there was no way she'd endure living any amount of time in a Brooklyn hovel. I spent several days a week working in a Rand McNally travel store, doing receiving in the stockroom and researching a place we could move that was affordable and had good writing opportunities. The Twin Cities of Minneapolis and St. Paul stood out. I'd been having trouble finding full-time work in Washington, D.C., because I hardly knew anyone. The Twin Cities boasted two of every-thing. Two daily newspapers. Two alternative newsweeklies. Even two city magazines. My twisted logic was that I'd have double the chance to succeed there than I would anyplace else. The cities had a large theater community, and I'd always been a bit of a theater buff, going back to my junior high school days. The Midwest location also proved more comforting to Nicole.

The first thing one must understand is that Minneapolis is far removed from the rest of the Midwest, both literally and fig-uratively. By car, it's a full six-hour drive from Chicago to reach the Twin Cities. That's far enough to discourage all but the most intrepid drivers from making it. In fact, most Minnesotans refer to their state as being part of the "Upper Midwest," a delineation that speaks to Minnesota and states west, such as the Dakotas.

Arriving in the Twin Cities by car, one is first greeted by the Old World look of downtown St. Paul. The tourism brochures like to point out that St. Paul sits on seven hills, "like Rome," but somehow the St. Paul state capitol building doesn't quite inspire the same awe as the Vatican. It was designed by Cass Gilbert, the Minnesota architect responsible for the Woolworth Building in Manhattan (one of my all-time favorite sky-scrapers), and the entire city exuded a rather genteel, eastern feel. The residents recount a laundry list of native sons and daughters who left town to find fame and fortune elsewhere, none more famous than F. Scott Fitzgerald, who grew up in the city's historic Summit Ave. district.

Continuing up the road, Minneapolis hits you like a slap in the face. The downtown of the larger of the two cities is, well, larger. Much larger, in fact. Tall glass skyscrapers accent what looks like a giant pie, but is actually the Hubert H. Humphrey Metrodome, where the Minnesota Vikings and Minnesota Twins hold center stage. Most of the buildings in downtown Minneapolis are connected by second-level "skyways," enclosed pedestrian walkways that shield workers from the bitter cold. Minneapolis is a city defined by water, and more than twenty freshwater lakes are within the forty-five-mile city limits. Several of these lakes are connected by canals to form South Minneapolis's popular "Chain of Lakes." You can rent a canoe and paddle out onto the lake, slowly gliding from one lake to another by way of the canals. Minnehaha Creek, a long, winding stream, meanders through the southern portion of the city before finally spilling into the surprisingly majestic Minnehaha Falls. During the winter, the lakes freeze over, and local kids take to the ice for games of hockey.

I knew to expect these things before I even arrived in the area. I had, after all, done pretty diligent research while working at Rand McNally. What I never expected was just how quickly and easily I'd settle in to life in the Twin Cities. Yes, it got colder than anything I'd ever experienced (including a record-setting negative-thirty-eight degrees Fahrenheit during my first winter), but I quickly grew accustomed to the weather—it was nothing that layered clothing couldn't overcome—and more importantly, the mellow almost utopian way of life among the people. I was a kid who grew up in an environment devoid of trust, and suddenly I was in a place where it was socially acceptable to write a personal check at the drive-through window of Burger King. This place was everything that New York wasn't. However, unlike places like North

Carolina, Virginia, and Washington, D.C., it was everything that New York wasn't that I *wished* it could be. It was nurturing. It was safe. It was trusting. Nobody seemed anonymous. Once I got past the passive aggressive nature and grating accents of the locals, I was hooked.

There was also a surprisingly large expatriate community from both coasts. These were people who reminded me of the kids I'd grown up with. They weren't the ignorant crackers I'd encountered in Virginia. They were the pseudo-hipster-nerd Jewish kids (with Italian last names) and cyberpunk-goth-hoodlum black kids that I only thought existed in the region that began in New Jersey and crossed New York out onto Long Island. Many of them had conspired with the local Minnesotans to form what would later be referred to as the Minnesota Mafia. A more apt term would be the Minnesota Media Mafia. It turns out that the Twin Cities was a fabulous stepping-stone to a career in journalism, particularly of the entertainment variety. Picking up a single issue of alternative newsweekly *Minneapolis City Pages* in 1997, you'd come across names that less than a decade later would be gracing the mastheads and pages of publications ranging from *Rolling Stone* to *Newsweek*.

I quickly settled into a routine the likes of which I hadn't had in my adult life. I adopted neighborhood haunts. I became known to my neighbors, and not just in the scornful way that Howard students were accustomed to being treated when they moved into apartments near campus. I had a real, adult *routine*. We were living in an enormous two-bedroom duplex apartment on Harriet Avenue in Minneapolis's Whittier neighborhood. We'd taken the apartment because it was one of the only ones that would allow us to keep our two dogs, both pit bull mixes who'd grown to unusually large size. The female, Dot, weighed about fifty pounds, while the male, Deebo, tipped the scales at more than ninety pounds. Our landlord didn't seem to mind the huge beasts. He was a jovial gay man who lived in the apartment upstairs, and paid about as much attention to us and other tenants as he did to repair work on the building (none in both cases). Our other neighbors were a couple of goth kids who regularly smoked some of the funkiest weed I'd ever smelled.

I had a neighborhood dive bar, the Red Dragon, where the bartender announced last call every night by banging a baseball bat on the bar. There were coffee shops and art galleries and theater companies that all were suddenly in my lexicon. The Muddy Waters coffee shop around the corner was a winter favorite, as it had SpaghettiOs on the menu. The entire city was both invigorating and liberating. I even started bird watching as a hobby, going so far as to purchase a *Sibley Guide to Birds* and keeping it handy near my desk in case an unusual species flew by. I was a square and loving it.

Life in Minnesota was also humorously unique. For example, it seemed like everyone, regardless of his or her income, owned a canoe. You'd expect it in the many suburban communities like Minnetonka and Wayzata, where houses often ran right up to the lakefront. But it was a surprising sight in the little nouveau bohemia of Whittier, where duplex apartments outnumbered single homes two to one. I found out about the maritime leaning of my neighbors during one of Minneapolis's infamous thunderstorms. Much of the upper Midwest suffered from routine summer thunderstorms that make storms on the

East Coast seem like light sprinkles. It wasn't uncommon for more than an inch of rain to be dumped on the city within minutes, backing up sewers and flooding streets. As luck had it, we lived only a block away from Lyndale Avenue, one of the lowest points in the watershed for the Mississippi River downtown. During one particularly violent thundershower, Lyndale flooded for more than a mile of its length with over a foot of water. Nicole was stranded on the opposite side of the Lyndale River, and called me from a coffee shop. I wandered over to the corner to see if in fact it wasn't possible to cross the flooded street. It wasn't, and local hipsters in canoes had already begun paddling up and down its course. One guy even let his pet snapping turtle go for a swim.

Water seemed to be everywhere even when it wasn't raining, which I found unusual for such a land-locked city. No matter where one lived or worked, one was within walking distance of a freshwater lake. The locals I encountered recommended I take advantage of the abundant wildlife in the city lakes and learn fishing. They had no way of knowing my skepticism about the pastime thanks to my almost cosmic failure to catch even a single fish during all those years on the pier in Coney Island.

Still, I was intrigued by the tales of foot-long northern pike being pulled from lakes daily in the shadow of downtown Minneapolis. I had to at least give it a try. I picked up the absolute least expensive fishing rod I could find at a local sporting goods store and walked over to the canal that connects Lake Calhoun and Lake of the Isles in Minneapolis's trendy Uptown neighborhood. With pierced teenagers on in-line skates and soccer moms on bikes whizzing behind me on the bike path, I cast my line into the shallow water. Within ten seconds, my pole began to jerk. I had gotten a bite! Once I put out of my mind the possibility that it was a crab tugging on my line in a freshwater lake, I began to furiously reel in my prize, tugging and pulling the line like it was a swordfish on the other end. The other fisherman nearby looked puzzled.

When the hook finally emerged from the water, dangling on one end was a real, live fish! I happily grabbed it and gave it a close examination. The fish was flat, and couldn't have been more than four inches from head to tail. A man who'd been angling about ten feet away walked over and chuckled as he congratulated me.

"Looks like you got a crappie there," he said. "That's a pan fish."

Yep.

"Pretty small though. It would take fifty of those to make a meal. You might as well throw that back."

He must've been out of his mind. My first catch, and within only seconds of casting in my line, and he expected me to throw it back? I kept that fish in my freezer for more than a year.

Nicole loved the city even more than I did. It was a place that held many of the comforts she'd been accustomed to growing up, but was also culturally interesting enough that I wasn't going stir crazy. My first job was as an editorial associate at a small environmental organization in Navarre, one of a dozen towns surrounding Lake Minnetonka in the western Minneapolis suburbs. They needed a science writer to contribute stories to their several regular environmental newsletters. I had no experience writing about science, but they gave me the job anyway—which seemed to be the way things went in Minnesota. Even if you didn't necessarily have the best experience for a job, if you displayed enough energy, employers were often willing to give you a chance. How very *not* New York!

It seemed like every writing job I applied for panned out, and I was surprised by the speed with which my writing career took off. I was soon gainfully employed in the theater community while simultaneously writing articles for a number of local and national publications. Within two years, Nicole and I had married, a few of my friends from college had gotten on the bandwagon and relocated to Minnesota, and we were beginning to look into buying our first home. I'd even become accustomed to summers of being eaten alive by mosquitoes, Minnesota's unofficial "state bird."

I had also made new friends who rapidly became as dear to me as many of the ones I'd left behind from my childhood. New friends like Michael, a witty guy from the New York area who was living with his girlfriend, a Minnesota native (I later found out that getting into a serious relationship with a Minnesotan was the primary reason coastal transplants ended up in the Twin Cities). Michael was the biggest bibliophile I'd encountered since my buddy Philip. It only made sense, since he was responsible for book reviews in *City Pages*. He visited New York when he traveled home for holidays to see relatives, but didn't seem to particularly miss the place. I understood the apathy. New York was becoming a distant memory for me, too, and I found my priorities changing. Did I really need to return home to be a success? I was doing well here, and now writing for publications back in New York from long distance. I didn't really need to be back in the thick of things, did I? I hadn't even caught a glimpse of my first pileated woodpecker.

That's when the call came. There was a job offer on the table. It was a good one. It turns out I'd impressed the right people with my writing. The only caveat: I would have to relocate back to New York.

• • •

"My God, it is so great living here!"

I'm not generally one to eavesdrop on subway conversations, but this one is too loud and too annoying to ignore.

"I mean, I could have gone to school at UCLA, but when I came here to visit, I just fell in love with the Village. Have you been to UCLA?"

The girl's friend shakes her head no.

"I mean, it's a beautiful campus, but Westwood Village is so boring compared to the Village."

These girls are white. And I mean *really* white. I've never robbed a person in my entire life, but I find myself suddenly tempted to harass the girls and their boyfriends just for being so smug. Instead, I simply plant my face back into my magazine and try to shut them out for the remainder of our subway ride to Coney Island. I'm on my way there to visit my aunt. It appears they're going there to take pictures and hang out. These Herbs never would've even stepped onto the subway, let alone taken the train out to Coney Island back before I left.

Unfortunately, New York City had not remained in a stasis while I was away. In fact, the changes in the city could not have been more revolutionary. In the time that I was gone, the city had been through two mayors, including its first African American one. By the time I returned, New York was at the pinnacle of the Giuliani administration, or as anyone who wasn't black liked to say, the city's Golden Age.

New York was no longer mired in violence like it once was. Giuliani's primary focus when he came into office had been to attack the crime problem by focusing not just on big crimes, but smaller, quality of life ones, such as vandalism and littering. He sparked a turnaround that many never would've thought possible only ten years earlier. There was no longer any graffiti on subway cars. In fact there wasn't much graffiti anywhere. This was a big transition from my childhood, when anything left unattended would bear a tagger's mark within twenty-four hours—I found it amusing that even delivery trucks bore elaborate tags on their sides as they drove down the street.

Violent crime had also taken a nosedive, and Times Square had been transformed from a modern Sodom and Gomorrah into a fanny-pack friendly city crossroads that actually attracted tourists. And by tourists, I don't mean people from Long Island and New Jersey. I mean the same fanny-pack wearing Midwesterners who once swore they'd never visit the Big Apple. They were arriving in droves. Some were actually living here. Imagine that, New York City as the new vacation and retirement destination of middle America!

I'd been a regular visitor to the city throughout the years I was away, but I'd never noticed these cultural changes. Those little things are easy to overlook when your stays are for days or weeks at a time. Now, they were right in my face.

Strangely enough, my old friends no longer seemed to be around. And not just because I had taken up residence in Queens this time out.

Mike:

Mike had been my closest friend since the Shooting, but we'd fallen somewhat out of touch during our college years. Mike attended CUNY in Brooklyn, where he studied pharmacy. During one of our conversations freshman year, I asked him why he was majoring in pharmacy when I'd never heard him mention any interest in it before. His response was simple, classic Mike.

"I looked it up, and the starting salaries are some of the highest you can get with just a bachelor's degree."

It made sense, but I was still skeptical of how long Mike would stay in a career he wanted to pursue strictly for money. I'd always promised myself I'd only do a job I loved. My rationale was that no matter how off kilter a profession, if one were good enough at it, one could make a decent living pursuing it.

We spoke throughout college occasionally. Sometimes, it would be nearly a year between conversations. Still, I always had the comfort of knowing Mike wasn't going to be moving out of his parents' house until he got married, and he seemed to have absolutely no interest in getting married anytime soon.

His parents, an old-school Italian couple who went so far as to buy a satellite dish so they could receive Italian language television stations, barely spoke any English, even though they'd lived in the United States for decades. I'd harass Mike for years about how his mom made him double-check that their silverware was still all there the first time I came to his house (when we were kids).

The pharmacy career actually proved successful, and Mike was able to earn a comfortable living, while still enjoying the benefit of having his mom make his bed for him well into his twenties. Mike flew out to Minnesota to be in the bridal party for my wedding, and he was excited I was moving back to New York—even though we wouldn't have much time to hang out due to his many side pursuits, including day-trading and executive producing independent films.

Mack:

Mack and I lost touch for many years after I left New York. When we finally did catch up, I learned he'd had a child right out of high school. The last time we spoke was in 1995, when he was planning to travel to Washington, D.C., to attend the Million Man March. I offered my apartment as a place to stay, and I was excited to see him. Unfortunately, he never made it.

I knew he was playing some college basketball out on Long Island, but during the last call I made to his house, whichever family member answered the phone said simply he "wasn't around here no more," and abruptly hung up.

Jerry:

My friend from Murrow, Jerry and I hung out quite a bit initially.

He even came down to Virginia a few months after graduation to stay with me. We waited tables at a retirement community in Williamsburg and hung out with friends in the evenings and on the weekends. Jerry and I drove several of my little Virginia crew up to New York for a few days, where we hung with David, Mike, and some of the other guys.

However, after Jerry returned to New York for good, we also lost touch. The word was he'd moved in with his girlfriend, who lived in Staten Island, and virtually vanished. Even David, his closest friend since Murrow, didn't have new contact info for him.

Louie:

My good friend from elementary school days, Louie ended up leaving New York as an adult. We lost touch long before that, shortly after I left for Virginia. Upon returning to New York, I ran into his mother one day while driving near Hinckley Place, and she told me Louie had gotten into "lots of trouble" while he was in high school. After he graduated, he'd joined the Navy, and he was stationed, ironically enough, in Virginia.

Louie got in touch with me when he was back in town on leave, and we met at Tottono's pizzeria in Coney Island and shared a pie. He told me his soon-to-be wife was back in Puerto Rico, and that he ultimately wanted to be living there with her. I wished him well, told him to look up my mom in Hampton since he was stationed nearby, and never heard from him again.

Jesse:

Mike was actually the last person to speak to Jesse, our friend from the Stranahan days who took me apple picking. Mike said one day they were hanging out shortly after high school ended when they got rushed by some Puerto Rican kids. Mike said he and the rest of the guys ran off, leaving Jesse to fend for himself. He'd seen him on the street a few times after that, but they barely spoke.

Chris:

Chris, the only other person present when Henry was shot, stayed close to Mike. Strangely enough, he and I would not speak again until 2001, but it's too early for me to tell that story . . .

The broken ties were not limited to my friends. Like the guys from the neighborhood, my family had long since scattered into the greater New York City metropolitan ether, taking up residence in places like New Jersey and Staten Island. My family had always operated in a rather strange fashion anyway. After Mom made the decision to move down to Virginia, it took me by surprise that in short order all three of my older sisters decided to make the very same move. It was surprising considering the almost constant conflict between Mom and my sisters when they were younger. Maybe marriage and family changes those feelings. Between the three of them, my sisters had twelve children, so there was a lot of family to consider.

I remember my family being apart more than being together. In fact, the only time Mom, Dad, my three sisters, and I were all together under the same roof was when we lived in Coney Island. By the time my little brother was born, my eldest sister had already gotten married and had had her first child.

That faded paradise by the sea was just that, a faded little paradise. What I thought of as our "house" was in fact a large duplex apartment that was part of a complex that shared an enormous grassy playground. I was only about four years old, so of course from my perspective the place was about the same size as the Brady Bunch house. I loved the fact that, being a duplex, it had two separate levels, something unusual that I would not bear witness to again until I visited the inside of my first brownstone in junior high school. Having a staircase to run up and down was a great thing, even though I fell down those stairs on multiple occasions. The place held a great deal of life, inside and out. In addition to the family, we had several pets. A parakeet whose name escapes me, eventually escaped.

Not so fortunate were a revolving door of family dogs. Mom had a limited amount of patience with canines. From her point of view, dogs were always playing dumb. They could, in fact, perfectly understand English from the time they were puppies. Therefore, if you instructed a new dog as so . . .

"Basil, don't you dare shit in this house when we're gone!"

"King, don't you dare eat any food out of the garbage!"

"Kenji, don't you growl at me when I try to take your food dish!"

. . . and if the dog did not implicitly follow your commands, then it was insubordinate and had to be sent to the pound. It was hard to get attached to dogs when you knew they had such ridiculous standards to live up to from their masters. It also didn't help that we had a tendency to get big dogs, seemingly the least likely to obey those commands.

In all fairness to Mom, some of those dogs were problem animals. King, for example, was a fabulously fit male German shepherd. Mom had a thing for German shepherds, and King was about as perfect a specimen one could find. Unfortunately, the dog almost immediately ingratiated itself to my eldest sister, Sheila. She became the only person whose commands he'd follow. He also took it upon himself to protect all things Sheila throughout the house. If anyone ventured too close to Sheila's bedroom door, King's forceful growl would turn you away. The only person who didn't take the toothy hint was my sister Sharon, and King tried to tear her face off for her ignorance. After that, the dog was too dangerous to have around the house. Dad, always the conscientious owner, took him to the nearest junkyard and let him loose. He walked out the door with King, and returned alone.

I remember never wanting to leave Coney Island. Why would I? Everything I ever wanted was there. We did our shopping at a nearby Pathmark, where Mom saved money for her family by purchasing tons of white-label no-frills goods. This was before I knew what no frills meant, so I couldn't be embarrassed about it. Astroland amusement park was within walking distance of our apartment. Of course, I was too young to go there by myself, and my sisters were only willing to drag me along every once in a while. But when they did, I felt like the luckiest kid on the planet.

Astroland was one of the last of what were once many amusement parks that lined the boardwalk of Coney Island. I could chart my juvenile growth by my own ascension through the gauntlet of rides there and in the nearby Wonder Wheel Park. The journey began at the Astrotower, the second tallest structure in all of Coney Island. (The tallest was the derelict shell of the old parachute drop, inoperable since the seventies.) The Astrotower was a small donut-shaped room that slowly rotated and rose to the top of a 275-foot tall cylinder. This ride was really nothing more than an observation tower providing an overview of Coney Island and a good perspective of the incoming elevated trains. You could even see Manhattan in the distance on a clear day. For me, it might as well have been the Empire State Building. I'd run around in circles counter to the rotation of the room, taking in my little kingdom and looking down at the ride that would one day be my greatest conquest . . . the Cyclone roller coaster.

I graduated to the Bumper Cars shortly after taking my first trip up the Astrotower. Of course, I could only ride in the cars with one of my older sisters, but it was exciting nonetheless. Sometimes, one of them would even let me grab the wheel and steer our car off course or into a wall, the trail of sparks from the conducting cables crackling overhead.

The Enterprise was the first of the big kids rides I got to experience. The ride consisted of about a dozen dangling cars suspended around an enormous metallic circle. It looked like a Ferris wheel lying on its side. Once the riders were locked into their cars, the entire wheel spun rapidly, then lifted off of the ground until it was vertical, and the spinning cars were looping riders upside down repeatedly. I was excited to ride this one. I'd always loved being a spectator, often from a distance, since people tended to spit from their cars at the crowd gathered below. I once caught a phlegm-filled spit wad right in the face.

Once again, because of my small size, I had to ride on my sister's lap that first time. As the cars began to speed up, and as the giant wheel lifted off, I smiled wide. I expected a feeling of weightlessness, but the centrifugal force kept us both planted firmly in our seats. About a minute into the looping I gathered up the strength to open my mouth, and fired a loogie out the side of the car. It was nice to be on the giving end for once.

The Wonder Wheel was a Ferris wheel unlike any other, and it took a while before I had the nerve to venture onto it. It towered more than one hundred feet above the boardwalk. Unlike other Ferris wheels, the Wonder Wheel's cars were suspended on tracks so that as they circulated around, gravity forced them to roll about randomly like mini roller-coaster cars. As your car swung out over the concrete below, you wondered whether this would be the day one of the cars detached from its track and plummeted to the ground. There was a certain fear of death when riding many of Coney Island's attractions. It made sense, considering how rusted, rotted, and worn most of them looked.

The Hellhole, or "H-Hole," as I was required to call it, was an unusual ride for its time. It was simply a large circular metal room. Guests entered the room and stood with their backs to the wall. There were no restraints or bars on which to hold. The room began to spin rapidly, the centrifugal force pinning the riders to the walls. When the riders were sufficiently stuck to the walls, the floor would slowly drop, leaving everyone suspended several feet in the air, stuck to the wall like insects. The first time I rode it, a fat woman across from me slid down with the floor as it dropped. I guess no amount of pressure was going to keep her stuck to a wall.

The Cyclone was the king of all Coney Island rides. It was also the last Coney Island attraction I rode. The wooden roller coaster was originally constructed in 1927 by the Rosenthal brothers, Jack and Irving. I doubt they knew when they commissioned the ride how much it would strike fear into the hearts of every young person in Brooklyn for decades to come. The Cyclone was the only ride I didn't try while we still lived in Coney Island. My first ride on it wouldn't come until my freshman year of high school. Even then, after having ridden countless rides at amusement parks up and down the eastern seaboard, I thought the Cyclone's reputation as a fearsome roller coaster was well deserved.

What made the Cyclone so unique was how violent and rough the ride was. Most wooden roller coasters contain twelve drops, each one gradually lower than the next. The first drop is always the steepest, and the most fear inducing. From there, riders are propelled around the track, the height of each drop causing a brief sensation of weightlessness followed by the sudden G-force of being compressed in your seat at the bottom of the drop and during each of the turns. The Cyclone contained all of those things, multiplied by five. During my first ride (at night), I witnessed riders being slammed against the sides of their cars on every turn. When we all stepped off, only a minute and fifty-seven seconds after getting on, people were complaining of having bruises and injuries. One man was bleeding from his face.

Later, I would do some research on the roller coaster and find out that the ride was indeed more violent than other wooden roller coasters. As it turns out, when the Rosenthal brothers commissioned Vernan Keenan to design the roller coaster in the 1920s, Keenan had very little to work with . . . literally. The plot of land on which the Cyclone was to be constructed was considered too small for a wooden roller coaster. Rather than cut down on the number of drops and turns, Keenan simply designed the coaster so that those drops and turns were steeper and sharper, enabling him to fit all 2,640 feet of track onto the smaller site. The first eighty-five-foot drop sends riders plummeting down at a sixty-degree angle, the steepest drop of any wooden roller coaster to this day. The ensuing ride can only be described as relentless as you are thrown up and down, side to side without even the smallest respite.

The Cyclone legend grew from the day the ride was constructed. Some of the stories are certainly true, while others are dubious at best. I heard that a man who was a mute since birth regained his voice on the Cyclone when he screamed, "I feel sick!" Charles Lindbergh said the ride was more thrilling than his trans-Atlantic flight. I heard stories of people dying on the ride, being tossed from one of their cars. In fact, the Cyclone has always had a sterling safety record among roller coasters, but this kind of hyperbole made it the stuff of juvenile legend. The Cyclone was Coney Island's ultimate male rite of passage.

It was our haunted house, skid row, and pirate's alley all rolled into one.

And now it was all the way on the other side of the city. It might as well have been the other side of the world. With my old crew of friends and immediate family mostly gone from my life, New York had become a very lonely place. Compounding this was the fact that I was living in Queens, a borough I'd only visited when traveling to and from the airport. Queens was the antithesis of not only Brooklyn, but New York.

New York has always been a city known for its walkability, but Queens is a borough where you have to own a car in order to be comfortable. The constant travel on the spider web of expressways, combined with the seemingly endless sprawl, makes living there more akin to Los Angeles than New York. Brooklyn and Manhattan are defined by their regimented grid of interconnecting streets. Queens streets have neither rhyme nor reason for anyone who doesn't live there. It is a borough where 43rd Street intersects 43rd Place, which is different from 43rd Avenue and not in any particular order. Nicole, who had grown up accustomed to driving, took to the new environment faster than I did. For me, I might as well have been moving to a completely new city. When Mackenzie was convulsing in Nicole's arms, I was worried I might get lost on the way to the hospital.

Gone was Prospect Park, that midborough Brooklyn icon that serves as a wilder, grassier substitute to Central Park. I considered myself a virtual Sherpa for being able to climb to the top of one of the park's largest hills with my friends. There were a couple of crazy-looking homeless guys at the top, and we almost broke our necks tumbling back down the hill to get away from them.

Maybe it's because so many people in Queens have yards, but there's no Prospect Park or Central Park equivalent. The largest public green space is Flushing Meadows Corona Park. It's a park in name only, with hardly a tree in sight, and dominated by huge structures for sporting events. Shea Stadium. The Queens Museum of Art. The tennis center where the US Open is held. I don't even like tennis.

The layout of the borough isn't the only thing that's different. Queens culture is also very different from that of Brooklyn. In Brooklyn, it's as though the entire borough looks toward Manhattan: The city is some kind of Shangri-La, a place one can eventually end up if one makes it. Even as deep within the borough as I lived as a child, simply peering down Flatbush Avenue would reveal the twin towers of the World Trade Center peeking above the horizon.

Queens has its back to Manhattan. Rather than forming a downtown, the portion of the borough nearest the East River is simply a jumble of elevated subway tracks, dark and forbidding at night, and industrial during the day. There's no Brooklyn Heights promenade or historic brownstone district; there is Astoria, a working-class Greek neighborhood. Queens residents look toward Long Island as an ultimate destination. Parts of the borough have easier access to Long Island than Manhattan, and communities such as Bayside can easily be confused with the suburbs. Queens residents drive to Roosevelt Field Mall in the suburbs to shop rather than ride the subway into Manhattan. The subways themselves are limited, with only three or four major routes piercing the borough, leaving large swaths of it without any subway service at all. Residents frequent an abundance of bowling alleys and park

their cars next to clapboard houses with carports. This wasn't
home. This was some foreign country. Returning here was like
starting from scratch.

There were some things that hadn't changed at all since I'd
left. I'd heard tales from Mom about housing discrimination,
but I now had an opportunity to experience it firsthand. It was
a nice reminder of days past when I'd speak to a landlord
about an apartment available in a neighborhood, like Astoria
or Forest Hills, only to arrive and have the landlord shocked
to discover I was black. There would follow a sudden
announcement that his or her son or daughter, who recently
(fill in the blank with anything from "returned from college"
to "moved back to the city from overseas") had instead
decided to take the apartment, so it was no longer available.
It was amazing how much family turmoil could occur in the fifteen minutes it took for me to hang up the telephone and drive
to an apartment.

We did eventually find a landlord desperate enough to rent
out his apartment to let us sign a lease. It was in Woodside, a
neighborhood sandwiched between Sunnyside and Jackson
Heights. Woodside's claim to fame is that it has an unusually
large population of expatriate Irish families living in the neighborhood. There are an abundance of bars bearing four-leaf
clovers and such, leaving me to wonder: when left to their own,
do all ethnicities buy into their stereotypes?

The apartment was a large one-bedroom with an eat-in
kitchen, and the price was right. It was also a convenient
twenty-minute trip on the #7 train to the center of Manhattan.
My stubbornness about my new environs eventually subsided,
and I found a new pizza place (Woodside Pizza), a new snack

spot (Lemon Ice King of Corona) and other new activities nearby to replace the ones I'd had in Brooklyn. It's not like I needed to revisit the useless aspects of my childhood anyway. I was an adult now. I had different priorities. Still, I did eventually find myself cruising around the old neighborhood in Brooklyn. I was hoping to run into the guy who handcuffed me to a fence, so I could pay him back for that dose of reality all those years ago.

• • •

Success.
Moderate success.
Failure.

Of the three, moderate success has always been the worst to me. To be a "moderately successful" painter means you only sell enough of your work to pay the rent, but have to wait tables in order to buy new clothes. A moderately successful chef only gets to run the kitchen at mediocre establishments at best, if he ever makes it past sous chef. To me, being a moderate success is much more painful than the bliss of utter failure or the rush of true success. The worst part is that a moderately successful person usually has such an unrealistically high standard of success that it can never truly be achieved.

Thankfully, it was something that I'd never have to deal with—or so I thought when we moved into our new apartment in Queens. I was on the fast track to writing stardom. The only thing that could stop me was *me*. And why would I ever dream of stopping myself from becoming the best? I'd stuck to my plan thus far. I still wouldn't touch any of the established vices. No hard alcohol (at the Red Dragon back in Minneapolis I only occasionally had a beer, or a piña colada during the summer months), no smoking, and no drugs. I was a faithful husband and a caring father, doting on my daughter as she rapidly developed from newborn to toddler. As long as I continued on that path, I knew only good would come to me.

And then Mackenzie's illness derailed all of that. The doctor tried to assure us her extreme reaction to the fever was common among some children. As he put it, "some kids simply don't deal well with fever. Fortunately, they tend to grow out of it."

They checked Mackenzie for any signs of brain damage, but she was fine. Her room in Lennox Hill Hospital in Manhattan even overlooked the East River, which was soothing, considering my little girl was sleeping in a plastic box for several days. When we finally returned home, my level of insecurity was off the charts. I was terrified of being left alone with my own daughter for fear something horrible would happen to her. After enjoying a nice period without regular thoughts of Henry's death, he was back on my mind on a daily basis, even visiting me in my dreams. The more I thought of him, the less comfortable I felt around my own family. It didn't help the situation that Mackenzie would spend the next two winters in New York wracked by febrile seizures. We brought her to the hospital a second time. After that, we became accustomed to a routine of putting her in a tub of ice water and doubling up her Motrin and Tylenol doses.

Happiness became unattainable. My writing career continued to move forward, but it wasn't providing me with the same joy it did before. I found myself turning away a number of assignments simply because I didn't have the energy to pursue them. Many of these were stories I would have jumped at the opportunity to write only a year earlier. My wife, meanwhile, had grown increasingly disenchanted with life in New York. It brought her down, she'd say, riding the subway into work every morning. She said the expressions on the faces of the other riders were looks of defeat. She was afraid that one day she would look as worn down as the women burying their faces in their copies of the *Daily News*. When a magazine at which I was working went out of business in 2000, I found myself considering something I never thought possible: leaving New York a second time.

Chicago seemed like the perfect substitute. Unlike Minneapolis, this was a major city in which I couldn't fall into a pattern of complacency or feel I was out of the loop. It was also less expensive than New York, so it wouldn't be necessary for me to work on so many projects. I would have liked to say that I'd miss my friends back in New York, but so many of the guys from the old neighborhood had long since vanished that it no longer mattered where I lived. I'd hear from them as often living in London as I would living up the block.

I'd decided to tell the story of the Shooting in print before even moving to Chicago. It had been on my mind as a possibility since I'd returned, but events like the Dorismond shooting had pushed me over the edge. I found a magazine that was willing to put my story in print and busily got to work on it. By the time we moved to the Ukrainian Village neighborhood on Chicago's near-west side, I'd completed a draft. It wasn't easy. The more I wrote about the Shooting, the more vividly the details came into my head. It was already an event that had been almost photographically seared into my brain, but seeing it written made it more real than I'd expected. I was uneasy.

Fortunately, Mike had become a much larger part of my life by then. When his day trading side project fell through, he found himself with much more time on his hands, and we began to speak on the telephone regularly. He provided counsel to me in what were increasingly becoming times of need. As it turned out, Chicago had numerous stresses of its own.

• • •

I could hear them off in the distance, their giggles and wisecracks just barely audible over the incessant questions being flung at me by the children. Whose children I have no idea. To me they're just various neighborhood kids on their bicycles who've come to gape at this marvel of physics.

"So, is that your car?" one of the youngsters asks, to which I respond with a quiet nod.

"Damn, that was a nice car too," remarks the other as my eyes glaze over and I listen ever more intently to the chatter in the distance. Mind you, the conversation I'm listening in on is no more substantive than the one my young charges have been engaged in. However, it's the police who are speaking, and the fact that their jokes are about my sudden misfortune makes their conversation much more interesting. I continue to stare at the wreckage and try to hold it all together.

My mind began breaking down long before my car ended up inserted in my neighbor's garage wall. We'd relocated to

Chicago from New York to save not just our psyches, but money. We'd saved a little already, but not as much as we'd hoped, considering our combined salaries. To me, that just comes with living in New York. You forfeit any chance of having a savings in exchange for the cachet that comes with dwelling in one of the greatest cities on earth.

The wife wasn't buying it. She's from Wisconsin, so I suppose her pragmatism was to be expected. She'd become worn out by the gravelly faced straphangers she shared space with while riding the crowded train to her nonprofit job in Harlem. She'd grown weary of the laborious work and the lack of pay, miniscule even when compared to work she'd done with comparable nonprofits in much smaller cities. And above all, she reasoned she just wasn't a New Yorker at heart.

Fortunately for her, Chicago, while large, was nothing like New York. New York was Wall Street and stocks, while Chicago was LaSalle Street and commodities. New York was wine, while Chicago was beer. Up until that point I'd viewed it (as did many other New Yorkers) as flyover country. The wife saw it as the bastard older brother of Milwaukee. Still, we decided on the city as a new home because it was (a) cheaper than New York, (b) large enough that I could still find meaningful and fulfilling employment as a writer and (c) just seventy-five miles up the road from her family in Milwaukee, a family she wanted to have much more access to our daughter.

Things began spiraling downward almost as soon as we arrived. Finding a suitable apartment was a chore further made difficult by my lack of knowledge of any of the city's neighborhoods. When the real estate broker pitched me on the sparkling clean three-bedroom occupying the top floor of a town house, I was sold on the picture perfect views of the Chicago skyline. I failed to notice the seedy nature of the neighborhood, which manned a border area that would have been a homesteader's fantasy in New York, but was just a marginal gang turf by Midwest standards.

I made a return trip to NYC soon after arriving. I had a number of writing assignments in flux that I didn't have the opportunity to finish before I'd left for Chicago. My wife dropped me off at the blue line El station at Damen and Milwaukee Avenue, where I'd catch the train to O'Hare for my flight. While waiting at the terminal gate for my plane to board, she called me on my cell phone.

"Hon, it's me."

What's up?

"We got into a car accident."

I began to panic. She said she'd been rear-ended while stopped at an expressway on-ramp. She said she and the baby were fine, and that I should go ahead to New York and not worry about it. She just wanted to let me know.

Of course, when I got to New York the details began to come out. The car that rear-ended her was an SUV, and it was going fast enough that it threw her car off the road and onto a mound of grass. The car crumpled enough that the back doors couldn't be opened, and while our daughter was unharmed, the shattering of the rear window showered glass onto her, and she was still panicked. My wife, meanwhile, had a minor pain in her neck that got progressively worse over the day. By the evening, she couldn't move her neck, and her mother had driven down from Milwaukee to help watch the baby. Oh, and the driver of the other vehicle was uninsured.

I cancelled my plans in New York and caught the next flight home. My wife informed me upon arrival that the car was considered beyond repair, so its value was being totaled out by the insurance company. I needed to go over to the garage where it was being kept and gather our belongings. When I stepped into the garage, my heart dropped. What had been our green 1997 Volkswagen Jetta was now a mangled pile of metal. The rear half of the car had collapsed like an accordion, and broken glass and debris covered the interior. I found it hard to imagine how anyone could walk away from such an accident, and I said a silent prayer of thanks as I gathered the broken compact discs from the backseat.

In the two weeks following the payout on our car, things finally began to settle down. We'd used the small amount of money left after paying off the car loan, and most of our remaining savings, to purchase a brand-new car. A 2001 Volkswagen Jetta. We went with blue this time, thinking the old car's green color made it cursed. I called my wife at her office.

Let's head over to Michigan Avenue after work today.

"I don't really feel like it," she replied. "It's been a long day, and I honestly just want to pick up Mackie, go home, eat dinner, and get some rest."

Are you sure? It's really nice outside today. Wouldn't be a bad time to walk to a couple of stores.

My subtle bribe didn't stick. She wanted to head home.

As is usually the case, we pulled into our driveway at about six PM. You enter the driveway through an alley. Par for the course for Chicago, and I began calling the network of alleys behind the many neighborhood townhomes the "second neighborhood."

I reasoned that every neighborhood in the city had two kinds of residents: porch dwellers and alley dwellers. There seemed to be a class distinction between the two. The porch dwellers, who usually didn't have the luxury of a back deck for barbecuing, were relegated to sitting on their front porches while their children played in the streets.

The alley dwellers all had back decks, and used them during the summer months for cookouts and parties. Alley children played more safely in the alleys because the speed bumps prevented cars from moving too fast. This led to temporary basketball rims taking up residence near garages all over town. There was a certain sense of security being an alley dweller, and the little surrogate community that had sprouted up in the alley behind the 2000 block of Huron Street provided quite a bit of relief from the stresses of daily life.

We scurried up the back deck to our apartment on the top floor. I looked out at the skyline of the city, the view that I used to convince myself that our apartment was worth it, despite the neighborhood. On Independence Day, the deck had provided spectacular views of the fireworks display downtown and in the surrounding neighborhoods. Chicago neighborhoods still knew how to launch serious fireworks, and sitting there on the deck recalled images of eighties Brooklyn. The spectacle also made me think of the Gulf War, as the light show was eerily reminiscent of the nighttime aerial assaults on Baghdad. The summer was winding down now, though, and within twenty minutes, we were all sitting at the kitchen table and munching on steaks.

Then came the explosion. All of the windows were open, so

the sound made us jump out of our seats. It was as though a bomb had gone off, and my first guess was that a gas line had blown up.

I'm going to go outside and see what that was.

"OK. But be careful," Nicole said as I made my way down the stairs. I stepped out of the front door for a rare appearance to the porch dwellers, who had all begun gathering in the middle of the street and glaring up and down the block looking for the source of the explosion. Most of them were shrugging and chattering in Spanish, and no one seemed to know what had caused the sound.

I headed back upstairs.

"Well, what was it?" she asked.

I don't know. You can't see anything out front.

"Well, maybe it came from the back?"

It didn't sound like it, but I'll have a look.

I stepped onto the back deck, where our neighbors on the adjacent deck had gathered and were speaking in panicked tones on their cell phones. I waved hello to them.

"Isn't that your new car?" one of them said, looking uneasily at the driveway.

I leaned over the banister and took it all in. My car was no longer in the driveway. Instead, it was firmly inserted into a twenty-foot wide hole in the side of my next-door neighbor's garage. Also squeezed into the hole was a late eighties Pontiac. Several police cars filled the alley, and several bike cops were pedaling up. One of the cops looked up and saw me.

"Is this your car?" he asked.

"Yeah!!!!!" I said, trying to hold in the pain. "I just fuckin' bought it!"

"Well, you'd better come down here," he said, as some of his associates tried to hold back laughter at the expression on my face.

To them, my reaction was that of a yuppie alley dweller mourning the loss of his shiny and cherished ride. They had no idea that this was the second accident to befall my family in as many weeks. They had no idea we'd relocated from New York in an effort to save, and that all of our savings had just vanished. They had no idea that had we been just twenty minutes later in arriving, my wife would've been crawling into the backseat to unfasten my daughter just at the moment of impact. They knew nothing of my daughter's health problems, and my increasing fear for her safety.

The cop explained there'd been a chase. The driver of the car had been trying to evade the police by driving backward down the alley at about fifty or sixty miles per hour. When he hit one of the speed bumps, he lost control of the car and slammed into our parked car, launching both of them into the wall of my neighbor's garage. One of my neighbors chimed in that it was some kind of gang dispute, and that the passenger had been firing a pistol out of the passenger side window. Another cop came walking up the alley with a handcuffed teenage Latino kid in tow.

"This is the driver," he said. "The other one got away."

Within an hour, it seemed like everyone who lived within ten blocks of us had come to gaze at the gaping car-filled hole in the garage. As the sun set, I was beginning to wonder whether people would set up a campfire and roast marshmallows. The whole thing took on a rather festive atmosphere. I wondered if the car in the wall hadn't been mine if I couldn't have joined in the festivities. My wife sat on the telephone with State Farm Insurance trying to convince them that *another* Volkswagen Jetta we owned had been hit in the rear and leveled.

After what looked like a lecture was given to the driver of the car in the backseat of one of the cop cars, he was taken out in handcuffs and turned to face me.

"I'm sorry I fucked up your car," he said, sounding about as sincere as an axe murderer being led to the chair.

The cop then led him out of the alley. On foot.

"They're letting him go," my neighbor Arthur, the owner of the garage, said matter-of-factly.

What are you talking about?

"That cop is dating the kid's mother. That's why they're not taking him to the station. I think he's taking him home to his mom." Arthur shook his head, cursed under his breath, and went to survey the damage to his garage, as I stood there mortified.

Winter was a struggle without the use of a car. We burned through our savings and incurred a monster debt paying for various rental vehicles. The insurance company decided not to total out this one, and we spent six months waiting for the car to be rebuilt. The Ides of March came and I learned my dad had cancer. Given, we all figured his emphysema would do him in sooner or later, the man chain-smoked as long as I could remember—even after his diagnosis he'd fire through a pack a day—but emotionally the news couldn't have come at a worse time for me.

Then there was the call from Mike. His father had been

diagnosed with cancer, and it was terminal. Within six weeks Mike's dad would be dead from one of the most painful, vicious bouts of lung cancer I'd ever heard of. I sat in my living room watching television one day, trying to take my mind off of the twisted joke that had become my life. A commercial came on, something about the fact that within one generation there wouldn't be enough food to feed the rapidly growing world population. I still don't understand why, but that's when I snapped. Suddenly, I couldn't breath. I broke into an intense sweat and fell onto my side and began to hyperventilate.

Nicole!

My wife came into the room and stared quizzically at me.

Help me!

"What's wrong?" she asked.

I couldn't speak. I couldn't breath. I was dying. My body had given up on me.

And all I could think about was the stupid car. Later, when I discovered I was suffering from severe anxiety, as well as depression, gastroesophegal reflux disease, and a few other things I never thought I'd have, I came to realize that the car had become a metaphor for my fragile psyche. My therapist explained it to me succinctly. When the kid "fucked my car up," he unwittingly fucked up my mind just as much by tearing away some of the last security barriers I had to keep the stresses of the outside world from overwhelming me.

But at this particular moment, while I'm lying paralyzed on my sofa with my wife standing over me, all I wish is that the kid had swerved a little to the right and fucked up someone else's car.

Part Four.

S uffering from anxiety and panic attacks does not necessarily constitute a breakdown. In fact, "nervous breakdown" isn't even a clinical term. It's a social term that describes when a person suffers from debilitating anxiety or depression. It best described what was rapidly happening to me.

I was proud of the fact that up to that point I'd rarely ingested any foreign substances. I'd never taken a puff of marijuana. I'd only drunk an occasional glass of wine at special events. I'd never even smoked a cigarette. I would only come down with a cold about once a year, and sometimes I'd go several years between any kind of illness. I now believe that that lack of foreign substances and illnesses worked against me. When my doctor prescribed the first of several medications to combat my anxiety and depression, I had no idea that every one of them would affect my system more like a virus than a cure.

Still, I had no choice. When the attacks came, they were debilitating. I spent two weeks after that first attack holed up in our apartment, unable to leave even to take out the garbage. I remained swaddled in a comforter, sweating and shivering, afraid that if I stepped outside a meteor would crash into my skull. It sounds ridiculous now, but that was exactly how I felt.

When I finally did manage to make it out of the apartment, I would only last for short moments before my breathing became labored and I'd have to rush back home.

When I made it back to work several weeks later, I had a panic attack a couple of hours into the day. I called my doctor and made an emergency appointment to see him. His office was only three stops away on the El, yet I still barely made it, almost fainting on the platform. When I did arrive, the sweating and breathing subsided enough for him to say I looked fine. Still, he began a battery of prescriptions. The first was the mildest he knew of: Paxil. Paroxetine, as Mike informed me the drug was known among pharmacists, is one of a number of selective serotonin reuptake inhibitors, or SSRIs. These drugs are a family of antidepressants that must be taken regularly for long periods of time in order to build up in one's system, as opposed to other, fast acting but habit-forming medications. I was to take the drug orally, and after a few weeks, I would supposedly feel better.

In fact, within a few weeks I was feeling worse. The labels on the outside of drug containers always list possible side effects. In my case, it was as though every single side effect was happening to me simultaneously. Only one ten milligram tablet of Paxil daily, and I was suffering from nausea, insomnia, shivering spells, diarrhea, and a complete loss of appetite.

So, my doctor prescribed alprazolam (Xanax), a controlled habit-forming substance I was instructed to take "as needed" for my attacks. Considering that an attack would come on every time I boarded an airplane, and that as a journalist I flew in a lot of planes, Xanax and I became close friends.

It didn't stop there. When my body failed to adjust to the Paxil, I was switched over to Effexor XR, another SSRI that left me confused, perpetually dizzy, and suffering from heart palpitations. Wellbutrin left me fatigued, sweaty, and suffering from headaches. A gray washed over my head and beard that year; doctors say stress has nothing to do with graying, and I once agreed. Not anymore.

Added to these treatments were medications for my now chronic stomach problems. There was the hyoscyamine sulfate I took once a day to treat cramping. Zantac (ranitidine) and Protonix were added to combat my constantly upset stomach. Prilosec was prescribed to handle the heartburn that was keeping me up at night when my insomnia wasn't. I'm not even certain why I was taking hydrocodone bitartrate, a narcotic pain reliever, but I certainly was taking that, too.

By the time my doctor had worked his way down the list to Neurontin, I was on the verge of giving up. It had been an eight-month journey in which I seemed to be going nowhere, and in the rare moments that I didn't feel high, I felt an irrational anger, or (as I would say in college), "I was pissed to the highest degree of pisstivity." The perpetual mental cloudiness made it difficult to concentrate, and I was finding it painfully difficult to formulate new story ideas at work. When the ideas did come, I struggled with even the most basic activities outside of the office. Simply walking down the street I'd sometimes stumble from one side of the sidewalk to the other, so badly was my depth perception thrown off. My productivity at the magazine plummeted, and my byline became an increasingly rare sight.

Surprisingly, Neurontin was the medication that finally

worked—without an abundance of side effects—and it wasn't even an anxiety medication. The drug is used to treat epilepsy patients, but one of its many off-label uses is to treat anxiety. I still felt terrible most of the time, but within a couple of months the anxiety attacks were down to once or twice per week, and the side effects were bearable enough that I could concentrate on other things. By the time I traveled to my cousin Leslie's wedding in New Jersey during the first week of September 2001, I had even managed to deal with the stresses of flying without resorting to the Xanax. Unfortunately, my marriage was beginning to flounder, and on the flight Nicole wept and expressed concerns about our being able to survive as a couple. During the long period of battling anxiety attacks and depression, the communication between the two of us had begun to deteriorate. Our apartment was a three-bedroom, and I'd begun spending increasing amounts of time in the third room alone, staring at my computer screen or lying quietly on a futon. The conversations we'd had in that room became increasingly tense as she began to press me for when I might be getting back to being my old self. I didn't have any answers, and I didn't have the patience to be questioned about it either, so I began openly wondering whether we belonged together at all. It left her shaken, but she'd remained quiet about it until this airline confrontation.

I was shocked and disturbed, but we both kept straight faces for the wedding. In fact, it was nice getting out and having the opportunity to see my family, and Leslie's wedding was beautiful.

• • •

September 11, 2001.

I get up out of bed and go to the bathroom. After returning to our bedroom, I turn on the television. An image of one of the World Trade Center towers is on the screen, and there is black smoke billowing from near the top. *Today Show* host Matt Lauer says that a plane has crashed into the building. As the newscasters debate the size of the plane that hit the tower and how such an accident could have occurred, another fireball erupts from the other tower. An instant replay shows that the plane that crashed into the tower was a big one. It looked like a 747. What on Earth was going on?

Every person in America can probably remember where he or she was on that fateful day, and despite my anxiety, I'm no different. I was about to go to work, but instead I spent the morning trying to verify that all of my friends and family who worked in or near the World Trade Center were safe. Mike worked just across the street, and my repeated calls to his cell phone went unanswered. The calls that did come to my telephone were distressed ones from friends and relatives asking if I'd heard from one person or another. When the first tower began to crumble to the ground, I leapt up and down pointing at the television, hoping that someone would step in and stop what I saw was happening. So many writers have used so many words to describe what transpired that day that I don't need to elaborate any more than this: terrorists crashed airplanes into the buildings that had been constructed the same year I was born; the towers fell, killing thousands, changing the city and the country once again.

When Mike finally did call, I was bordering on hysterical.

He recounted in chilling detail how he'd emerged from the subway terminal at the foot of one of the towers after the second plane hit. He was part of the large crowd that ran for their lives as the towers collapsed. He'd choked on dust and soot, and escaped into a subway tunnel where, of all people, he ran into Chris, who was there with me the day Henry died. It turns out Chris worked in one of the World Trade Center towers, and managed to escape after the first plane struck the building. He was walking out onto the street just moments before the building toppled to the ground. The two hugged and walked back to Brooklyn together, bloody and covered in ash. I spoke to Dad, who said confetti and smoke were floating past the windows of his apartment in Fort Greene, Brooklyn.

By the time I lay down for bed at the end of that long day, I'd managed to locate all of my friends and family. Even those who were in the buildings had managed to escape safely. It was the most tension-filled day I'd experienced in more than ten years. While manically trying to find people, I'd forgotten to take my anxiety medication. As I closed my eyes and fell asleep, I realized I had no desire to take a pill. I felt fine. I felt relieved. Ironically, I never took another pill for anxiety or depression ever again. I suppose disaster can be the most potent, if strangest, medication of them all.

• • •

Why would a person want a reminder of the worst day of his life? That was the logic I used to explain why Chris and I had never spoken to each other after Henry's death. The last time we saw each other was in the hall outside my apartment as the police ushered him away. He smiled at me, a comforting "everything is going to be all right" smile. It didn't soothe me in the least, but I appreciated the gesture.

Chris lived on the same block as Mike, and though the two remained close friends, after the Shooting he and I deftly managed to avoid one another. After a while it was as though we weren't even trying to dodge each other; our bodies had just changed frequencies to a point where we'd never be in the same place at the same time. Even the telephone couldn't get us together. If I called Mike and Chris was around, we'd greet each other through Mike. It wasn't that I didn't want to see Chris. I just didn't know what to say in those initial days and weeks following the Shooting. Before I knew it, those days and weeks had morphed into years. When September 11 rolled around, Chris was working with Mike's older brother at a computer company located in the World Trade Center. A week after the buildings fell, I rang Mike and asked him how he was doing. Mike said he was feeling much better. He said he was feeling lucky. Then I asked him how Chris was doing.

"He's good. He's still shaken up, but he's fine."

I explained to Mike that I wouldn't mind talking to Chris and a few other friends who had survived the disaster for a possible story in my magazine. Mike thought it was a good idea, and said he'd tell Chris and some other friends right away and see if they were up for it. He got back to me a few hours later.

"Umm . . . I don't think Chris is going to be up for it."

I wasn't surprised, considering the trauma of what he'd endured. But Mike's voice and manner sounded like something more was there, so I decided to pry. I asked him, was there something else wrong?

"Well, he just said you didn't have anything to say to him all of these years, and now you called him up when you wanted something."

I was shocked. I thought Chris didn't want to speak to me for many of those years. During one occasion, when I called Mike to say hello years ago, Chris was sitting in his house. I asked Mike to put him on so I could say hi. When Mike told him I was on the phone, he immediately stepped out. I took it as a sign we had to remain at a safe distance, and decided not to push the issue any further. This reaction felt as though it was coming out of nowhere. Once again, I decided not to push the issue. Mike said that if he even brought up the subject of Henry's death, Chris would change the subject. He had less of an interest in talking about it than I did, if that is at all possible.

In the end, it was Mike who brought the two of us back together. Mike had always mentioned how he, Chris, and some other mutual friends were addicted to playing PC games in the evenings and on weekends. We were all huge fans of the video game *Warcraft*, a strategy game in which rival factions (each controlled by a person online), engage in digital skirmishes to eliminate their enemies. When *Warcraft 3* arrived on the PC, all of us had copies of the game, and Mike suggested we meet online for an occasional match. It was interesting having that first correspondence with Chris after all of those years be a simple "What's up?" typed across the bottom of a computer monitor. Still, at least we were communicating again. I couldn't blame him for not talking, because I hadn't exactly been anxious to reminisce up to that point either.

• • •

Unfortunately, my father's health was getting progressively worse. His doctor had given him no more than six months to a year to live, yet Dad managed to struggle on for another couple of years, enduring the removal of his larynx and being completely bedridden those last agonizing weeks.

I remember vividly the day when Mom left Dad. We were still living in Coney Island, and I couldn't have been more than four years old. Dad had left for work, and within minutes of his walking out of the door, Mom began packing and moving our things out of the house. I wondered how terrible it was going to be for Dad to arrive home from work that evening and find his family had moved. I really liked Dad, even though he wasn't around much, and part of me wished I could have stayed with him. It wasn't until much later, when we'd moved to Hinckley Place, that I found he'd in fact been physically abusive to Mom.

I came home from school to Mom sitting in the kitchen wearing dark sunglasses. She pulled them off of her face to reveal a black eye.

"You see?" she said. "This is what your father did. Do you still think that he's so great?"

I rarely saw Dad, but the occasions in which I did were very exciting for me. When we went fishing on the Coney Island pier. When I got to ride around with him in his van. Dad was a charter bus driver for old rock-n-rollers like Jerry Lee Lewis, and he always told me the stories of driving famous musicians around the country. Once, when a church group chartered a bus to Myrtle Beach, South Carolina, he even let me come along. For two weeks I spent my days boogey-boarding on the beach and my nights enjoying the fish fry with the church group.

While Dad's bus driving seemed glamorous, I later found out his reasons were purely pragmatic; it was a rare job in which he could be paid in cash, off the books. Dad was a simple man that way. When one of his teeth bothered him, he scoffed at the idea of going to a dentist, instead removing pliers from a drawer and pulling the tooth out himself. Eventually he'd pulled so many of his teeth that it changed the way he spoke, and he would slur certain letters. It was no surprise, then, that he smoked more cigarettes than ever after being diagnosed with cancer. I'd visit him at his tiny apartment in Brooklyn, and between hacking coughs he'd pull out a cigarette and shoot a wink my way, as though asking me not to tell his doctor. I told him he was just hurting himself, and he'd nod and seem remorseful in between drags.

Eventually, things got so bad he could no longer survive on his own. Walking was such a laborious task that he could no longer navigate the stairs of his apartment building, and the chemotherapy and radiation treatments left him perpetually weak and in pain. He moved down to Virginia to be cared for by his sister for those final months. In February 2003, my dad finally died. He was sixty-one years old. He was among the elder of his many siblings, and several of his brothers had died years before. Uncle Kenny died of cancer in his fifties, and Uncle Tunk died of complications from AIDS at a similar age. Considering the lifestyle my dad led, I thought it was impressive he'd made it so long.

The trip down to North Carolina for the funeral was surreal. I hadn't been to this place since I was a child. My aunt Martha still lived on the farm, but Uncle Buddy had long since passed away. Before he died, he'd brought them into the modern era, and their house now sported a working bathroom complete with toilet, tub, and shower. I still stayed at a hotel.

The funeral was a solemn occasion for me, made more difficult by the fact that I had to speak in front of an assemblage of my family members. I'm generally not one to shy from speaking in front of a crowd, but this was different. These were family members on my father's side whom, for the most part, I hadn't seen since I was a child in Brooklyn. I was uncomfortable standing in front of them. But I knew none of my sisters would step up and speak. My eldest sister, Sheila, didn't even want to view the open casket. Instead, she sat outside the church.

I'd pulled out my journal during my flight and fashioned the best eulogy I could under the circumstances.

I'm a writer by trade, so it's strange that I'm up here today struggling with what to say. What words to use. It's even stranger that I'm up here at all making these remarks, because of all my siblings, I think my father and I had the most difficulty communicating.

Despite that, I learned a lot about James Powers over the years. I learned that while he wasn't always quick to say it, he was a man who dearly loved his children. A man who dearly loved all of his family.

No matter how difficult things got for him, he displayed an unshakable will. A will to go on. A will to live. It was a will he displayed right up until the end.

I will truly miss my father, because as much as days like today are inevitable, I don't think I was quite ready for it to come. I know that I wasn't ready to have him out of my life. God bless his soul.

To this day, I felt I could have said so much more. I could have talked about the many events and people that shaped my father's life. I could have talked about the sacrifices he made for his family, being the paternal figure for his many younger siblings after their father passed away. But that short eulogy was all I had the energy to write. Emotionally, I was getting tired. I was tired of trying so hard. I was exhausted with making so much effort only to have my life fall apart. I wasn't sure how much more of this I could take.

After the funeral service, we drove to the plot of land where Dad was to be laid to rest. They slowly lowered his coffin into the hole, and we took turns dropping flowers into it. I looked to the side of Dad's new home, and noticed the adjacent tombstones. One read "Kemp Willis Powers." His father. Next to it was another that read "Kemp Willis Powers." His grandfather. Two men who shared my name whom I'd never met.

● ● ●

You need to let go of all of this baggage that you're carrying around with you.

A more baffling suggestion has never been made. Letting go of it all sounds a lot easier than it really is. My personal views on the subject of "letting go" were largely dictated by film. In movies from *It's a Wonderful Life* to *Fight Club*, the protagonist always comes to his stunning revelation, then lets go of all of his emotional burdens and begins to live a more fulfilling life. A sort of Scrooge-like process, with the emotional shackles being the only barrier between that person and happiness.

What a load of nonsense. For me, letting go of the worries and feelings of obligation regarding Henry's death resulted in an almost immediate unraveling of my entire life. The speed with which it happened was astounding. Within the course of a single year, I'd destroyed my marriage, alienated most of my closest friends, derailed my career, and brought myself to the verge of bankruptcy. It was like a work of art. Coming on the heels of my prolonged bout with anxiety attacks, it was as though I'd fallen from a building and landed hard on the pavement below, only to have a sinkhole open and drop me into a sewer.

"It's like all of us walk around with this membrane surrounding us. This membrane is what keeps everything out, all the stresses and problems of the world."

This is my shrink talking. I'm embarrassed even to be sitting with the guy, my first therapist since sitting with Keith as a child. This shrink wasn't court appointed, but I feel like the sessions offer just as little in the way of resolution for any of my problems. He continues and tells me how my own personal membrane has shredded, and as I walk down the street, I can't help but find myself trying to empathize with the plight of every person I pass. This is the root cause of much of my anxiety, he says, and on this one point he may be right.

When I drive past the Cabrini Green housing projects en route to work, I look at the burned-out windows, see the families out front and wonder how they got to this horrible station in life. I begin to fantasize, seeing this patriarch's dreams shatter after numerous failures. I see him promise his family they'll only spend a few months in their new home, until they get on their feet. His efforts to get back on his feet include attempts at getting union work at an area manufacturing plant and taking courses on starting his own business. All of these endeavors are fruitless, and before you know it he has more children to feed. He eventually gives up, leaving his wife and the children to their own devices. The cycle continues as the teenagers grow up in the oppressive environment never knowing life beyond the project walls. I see all of these things in my mind's eye, and it fills me with a melancholy that ruins the rest of my day. Rinse, repeat, and that's my schedule for the week. It makes me so depressed, because I find myself wondering how far from a similar fate I might be.

I hadn't even realized how emotionally distant I'd become from all of my loved ones. My wife, my family, and my friends were increasingly on the periphery of my thoughts. I was feeling better from the standpoint that I was no longer medicated, and not suffering from any panic attacks—I'd even stopped having the nighttime visits from Henry in my dreams, though in many ways I missed them. (While the constant nocturnal reminder of my deed had been an emotional scar, it was also in many ways an emotional bandage.) But in terms of the person I now was, I'd become a funhouse mirror version of the person I'd once wanted to be. I'd achieved the moderate success I so wanted to avoid in my career, and was feeling all the more the failure for it. My already strained marriage was now unraveling in fast-forward. Within just a few months of moving into an upgraded apartment in Chicago's ritzy Old-Town neighborhood, we would be separated. We would spend the next year making several failed attempts to reconcile before finally calling it quits for good. I think she would be much better off without me anyway, as my self-loathing is bound to bring down anyone who comes within earshot of me.

I'd also taken to getting caught up in many of the vices I'd spent so many years proudly avoiding—if I had to let go, what better way to do it than over a drink or five? My preferred libation almost immediately became scotch. I'd drink it straight up or mixed with ginger ale. Neat or on the rocks. Single malt or blended. You'd think I had become a scotch expert, and not just because I'd attended a scotch seminar for a story I once wrote on Johnny Walker.

I went from being a guy who preferred to spend most evenings at home with a book or watching a movie to a person who couldn't exist after hours anyplace other than a bar. When left to my own devices at home, my feelings of self-loathing and bitterness would became overwhelming. At a bar, I was distracted by the conversations of people whose lives seemed even more screwed up than mine. Misery does indeed love company, especially when that company has it rougher than you. For a period of several months, not an evening went by when "hey, at least I'm not that guy," wasn't the thought that punctuated my evening. Fortunately for me, Chicago had enough hard-luck cases to go around. Also, at least I wasn't drinking at home . . . when I could stand to be there.

"So where are you from?" the guy at the bar asks.
New York.

"No shit? What part?"

New York.

"Oh, the *city*?" he says, looking perplexed.

Yeah. Well, Brooklyn to be exact.

"Damn, I'm just pretty surprised. No offense, but you New York guys don't tend to leave your city very much. When you do, you don't come here."

He had a point. I'd come to Chicago to avoid coming full circle back home too early, and instead I'd gotten into the bitter, self-deprecating routine anyway, just in a different place. I was treading water, and I needed a change. However, this time out I didn't know what that change could be. I felt like I had nowhere else to go. I no longer had the desire to do anything. I no longer wanted to try to move forward, because there was nowhere else for me to go but down. I had no one even to seek out for advice. Nothing to give me solace. That is, nothing except the next glass of scotch. I knew it was easy to step off of the path, but I never realized how easy it was to end up lost in the woods once you stepped off.

I wonder what kind of advice Henry would have given me in a situation like this? He was always good at finding the positives in any situation. He'd have been a wonderful drinking buddy right about now. He had counseled me on girls and bullies. I wonder how he would have counseled me on getting over him. I wonder if he would have started talking about God, and whether I would have immediately been repulsed by his reliance on faith or religion, or empowered by his blind devotion to it. Even at fourteen years old, Henry was a man of faith. He was walking a righteous path. For a while, at least, so was I.

• • •

Ever since the day Henry died, I've been overcome with questions. Questions about what would have become of my life had some subtle changes taken place on that day. I honestly feel that, given the circumstances—loaded guns, unsupervised, rambunctious teenage boys—such an accident would have been inevitable. But the number of possible scenarios was staggering. I could have pointed the gun at my own head. Then Henry or Chris might be writing a story about the years spent trying to recover from having watched their friend blow his brains out. Or Chris, Mike, or some other friend could have been at the end of that barrel. No telling what the familial response would have been, and I could've been sent to jail. If so, I could've very well emerged a hardened criminal. At one time or another I've replayed those alternate scenarios in my head, searching endlessly for the one that had a result that would be less grim, would leave me less adrift.

Scenario number one: Mike dies.

I don't recall exactly how long before Henry's death Mike and I had been playing around with the gun. It was in the kitchen of the apartment. I'd just handed him the .38 pistol, he'd marveled at its weight, then handed it back to me. That's when I decided to play the "Russian Roulette" game. I pretended to insert the bullet into the chamber, then aimed the gun at Mike. He immediately dropped cowering to the floor as I pulled the trigger the first time to a loud click.

"No, please don't!" he screamed, half-laughing as he grabbed my left leg. I point the gun at him again, and he both laughed and closed his eyes. I didn't even pull the trigger. I just laughed, then took the gun away and returned it to my mom's room.

But what if . . .

When I pulled the trigger I had made the same fatal mistake that I did with Henry later? The hammer cocks and fires, and the bullet goes right into Mike's eye. He falls to the floor, and I'm left there stunned. It's just the two of us, and in that moment I am all alone, panicked and unsure of what to do.

Another ten minutes goes by before I can muster up the courage to call anyone. I call my mom first, telling her I've made a mistake and shot Mike. It's Mom who calls the police, and they arrive before she does, they arrive to the gruesome scene of Mike's body slumped lifeless on my kitchen floor.

It's impossible to explain what has happened in any way that's acceptable to anyone. There were no other witnesses to the tragedy, and it's impossible for anyone to believe I didn't mean to shoot him. His parents are inconsolable, as is his older brother. I'm sent to juvenile detention until my eighteenth birthday.

Scenario number two: Chris dies.

Instead of pointing the pistol at Henry's head, I point it at Chris's. The same awful thing happens. The trigger is pulled. The hammer snaps. The gun explodes. Chris dies despite Henry's best efforts to save him. I'm too paralyzed with shock to do anything. I'm useless, and Henry is a hero. He looks at me as the police question us in the hall, and his eyes beg a simple question: why?

I never see Henry again, except in court, when he has to testify. Chris's grandmother and brother are there, and their cold stares pierce through to my soul. By the time the judge sentences me to ten years, I'm almost relieved to be getting out of that courtroom.

Scenario number three: The Shooting happened today.

This is the question that has popped into my head every time I hear a news report about young children and guns. Unfortunately, there is more than enough of them to keep the idea in my head. The ones that affect me the most are when the children are particularly young, and the question is raised about whether to charge a fourteen-year-old, a twelve-year-old, an *eight-year-old,* as an adult. It's as though today a child is considered liable after he speaks his first words.

I have no doubt that had the Shooting occurred today, I would have been given a mandatory prison sentence. That's just the way things are now. You commit a crime, you pay the price. "Zero tolerance" is a harsh term to me, made harsher by the fact that I only missed its implementation by a few years.

Scenario number four: I die.

The only scenario that offers me any comfort. I playfully point the gun at Henry, then as he leans back and puts his hands up, I turn it to my own head and pull the trigger. The pain is only momentary when the gun goes off. I fall over, and as my vision goes, the last image I see is Henry's sobbing face leaning over me, screaming.

Henry goes on to marry his girlfriend, and they end up having four children. After flirting with the idea of college, he decides his true calling is to become a firefighter. It's a noble profession for a noble guy: it makes sense Henry would be in the business of saving lives. He's hailed as one of the heroes of September 11, a veteran firefighter who manages to lead several terrified civilians through a smoky staircase and out of the building before the first tower comes crashing down. One of those people is Chris, someone he hasn't seen since his junior high school days. Henry and Chris have fallen out of touch, mostly because of the discomfort of being reminded of the terrible event when I killed myself, but this occasion brings the two old friends together again. Henry invites Chris over to dinner.

Mom handles my death terribly. She had no idea that I was even touching her guns when she wasn't around. Now her eldest son is gone, and she has no explanations. Why did I do it? Did I mean to kill myself? Was I unhappy? I wish I could somehow materialize to give her the answers she craves. To let her know it was a stupid accident and it never should have happened. But I'm dead, so she'll just have to have those questions in the back of her mind. At the very least, my stupidity didn't get anyone else hurt.

And just what if Henry hadn't died on my floor that day? Then who would I be? So much of my personality, so much of what I'd like to believe is good, can be directly attributed to that single mistake, and my attempts to atone for it. As frightening as it might sound, would I have been a worse person today were Henry still alive? Does even thinking it make me a terrible person?

● ● ●

Contemplating suicide is a terrible thing that's difficult to admit. It's even more taboo when you're black. The common lexicon states that black people simply do not commit suicide.
Ever.

Under any circumstances.

Even if they grew up around only white people. Suicide is just one of those things that is determined to be a whites-only burden. It's also a great equalizer in the black psyche. It's as though we say to ourselves "yeah, white folks have all of the power in this country, racist cops harass us all of the time and we have to endure discrimination and racism at the hands of white people from the day that we're born till the day we die . . . but at least our kids don't commit suicide. Heh. Heh." It's like God is getting even with white people by afflicting The Man's kids with a desire to off themselves at an early age. And for the silliest of reasons. For being too fat. For being picked on at school. For not getting into the college of their choice.

Black people love life too damn much for suicide. It's why a generation of black comedians has been able to make a living peddling the cliché about blacks in horror films. The second the scary music starts, the black person would get the hell out of Dodge. It doesn't matter how many traumas have happened to us over the course of our lives. A traumatic life is still better than being dead.

In reality, black people do commit suicide. The truth that is never discussed is that the denial of mental health disorders is as large an ailment among African Americans as the disorders themselves. In recent years, the suicide rate among black men has nearly doubled. Some studies have concluded it's the third leading cause of death among black men between the ages of fifteen and twenty-four. It's still much lower than our white counterparts, but thoughts of suicide do occur among black men. Sometimes, things feel so hopeless we want to end it all.

I didn't know this when I first began to think about ending

my own life; I felt like I was alone among black men in the world for having these thoughts. The memory of my intense medication, the strains of my marriage, the death of my father, and the general feeling that I had somehow fallen from grace had already inspired a slow suicide within me, as evidenced by the self-destructive behavior in which I had begun to engage: heavy drinking, fornicating, and confrontational behavior just to name a few. But gradually my thoughts began to turn to a more literal desire to no longer walk this Earth. I had come to a point where things felt hopeless. It seemed like I would never be happy again, like I would always remain a social leper, struggling with anxiety and depression. I had hoped writing about Henry's death would be a cathartic experience. Instead, it had the opposite effect.

My tiny failures, both personally and professionally, began to feel like they were larger and larger. One of my first stories to get killed got killed then. As a journalist, I had always prided myself on the fact that I'd never missed a deadline, and not a single one of my stories had ever been killed. I once spoke to a group of high school students interested in pursuing careers in journalism, and I pointed out keeping deadlines as the key thing that separated routinely employed writers from those who would never be able to get regular work. I never surmised I was the best writer around. In fact, I personally knew people who I believed were better writers than I was. However, I also knew those same people who wrote so well could never perform under the pressure of a deadline. If it were a freelance assignment, forget it. They'd just vanish.

I, on the other hand, thrived under the pressure of deadlines. My perfect track record also instilled a certain arrogance. I

don't even remember what the first story was that got killed, or
the reason why it wasn't going to run. I know that it was a freelance piece, and I know that when the editor called and told
me that the piece wasn't going to work, and that they were
going to pay me my fifteen percent kill fee, I hung up the
phone shocked and devastated.

From that point on, every tiny letdown became an ominous
sign in my own mind. Just like Mackenzie's inexplicable illness, my health problems, and everything else, this was tied
to something larger than me. It was something I had no control over, and that frightened me. Waking up in the morning
had become a terrible chore, because I didn't want to face
whatever new failure the day held. Eventually, this feeling of
burden turned into a feeling of exhaustion. I was tired of everything. Tired of trying so hard to no avail. Tired of thinking
about friends and family who were gone and whom I would
never be able to see again. Tired of wondering where I was
headed in my life, when just a couple of years earlier I could
have provided a script that described in detail everything I
planned to do until I was fifty, broken up into five-year
intervals.

But how could I kill myself? In what way could I stand to
die? Turning a gun on myself would be such a terrible cliché
that I couldn't stand the idea of seeing the ironic nature of my
demise being pointed out in some newspaper or magazine
article. Slitting my wrists wasn't about to happen—I was still
afraid of needles, so there was no way I was going to take a
razor to my own skin. A drug overdose seemed feasible, but
part of me wondered whether my period of extreme pharma-
ceutical use might somehow have made me less susceptible to

a sleeping pill overdose. I'd have a hell of a time explaining that one to Mom if it didn't work.

Just realizing I was thinking of ways to end my own life should have been enough to send up a red flag, but it wasn't. When I was working on stories that required travel, I no longer experienced extreme anxiety when flying. Quite the opposite. I was now experiencing an incredible calm. Perhaps it was because every time my plane lifted off the ground, I secretly hoped it would come crashing down. That would handle all of my problems for me. They would all float away with the gaseous fumes of the explosion.

A small family of birds took up residence outside our apartment window in Chicago. They were American Kestrels. I recognized them from my *Sibley Guide to Birds*. I'd never seen Kestrels in Minnesota though. I did finally catch sight of that pileated woodpecker shortly before I left, but the only raptors I saw were larger birds like bald eagles, horned owls, and various kinds of hawks.

Kestrels were different. They were the tiniest of all the falcons, smaller even than a pigeon. Their blue bodies made them stand out as they darted around the building. There were three of them, two males and a female. I saw them on an almost daily basis for several months. Those birds may have saved my life.

They helped me remember. I began to remember New York, but in a different way than I ever did before. Usually, the first image that popped into my head when I began to reminisce was Henry's coagulated blood on the floor outside of my bedroom. Those birds made me think of other things. Things I had long since forgotten amid the constant thoughts of death. I began to remember the butterflies. One of the most wonderful things about Prospect Park was the butterflies. It turns out the park was a haven for the large Monarch butterflies, their wings a bright orange to warn predators of their poisonous nature. Every spring, I'd wander up and down Caton Avenue along the southern end of the park, surrounded by hundreds of the butterflies. I'd hold out my hand and one would occasionally land on me.

Brooklyn had been such a beautiful place at times. It had filled me with such wonder. I remembered my uncle Kenny assembling his models. Kenny was Dad's brother, and long after Mom left Dad, Kenny would come by to see how she was doing. Kenny wasn't a violent man, and he took particular umbrage at Dad's having been physically violent with Mom. Usually when he visited, he would sit down for a few hours and work on assembling a scale model of a clipper ship. The model ships amazed me because of their detail, and Uncle Kenny amazed me even more for having the steady hand and patience to sit there and carefully place all of the tiny strings and components in their perfect spots, constructing models so lifelike they could have leapt right from the movie screen. His clipper and pirate ships eventually decorated our entire apartment on Hinckley Place. They sat at the top of every cabinet in the house, each one more ornate than the next. For the longest time, all I could remember from that apartment were the roaches. Now I was remembering those beautiful ships.

I remembered the first cassette tape I bought with my own money. I got it at a small music store a block off of Flatbush Avenue. It was Big Daddy Kane's album *Long Live the Kane*.

It was 1988, the same year that Henry died. I remember getting the tape and playing it until it almost broke. I had memorized every word to every song on the album, and could dance along step-by-step with Kane's backup dancers when the video for the single "Ain't No Half Steppin" aired.

I remember going to see *The Last Dragon* with my sister at the Duffield Twin movie theater in downtown Brooklyn. It was 1985, and at that time there was not a better movie in the world. It had everything. It had Vanity, the most beautiful woman on Earth. It had black people doing kung fu. It had Bruce Lee. It had the fresh soundtrack. During one of the opening scenes in the film, the main character, Leroy, is watching Bruce Lee's *Enter the Dragon* in a seedy movie theater in the ghetto. He sits there engrossed in the film as the other patrons smoke weed, drink, and raise an overall ruckus. The comedy of that moment was lost on me then, because the Duffield audience perfectly mirrored the audience in the film, complete with weed, booze, and shouting. It was only now that I recognized it.

But more than anything else, I was remembering when my daughter was born at the hospital in Queens. Her mother was unconscious from the drugs given to her before the C-section, so it was pretty quiet as I sat there holding Mackenzie in my arms in the operating room. Her eyes were closed, but I knew she could hear me as I welcomed her into the world. How much I would regret not seeing her grow up. Not seeing her do all of the things I knew she could. Not being there to support her when I knew she would need me. For all of my myriad failures, she was not one of them. In fact, she was my greatest success, and I wanted to see that success come to fruition.

• • •

An Open Letter to Henry:

Hey man, how's it going? It's been fifteen years since you left, and the time has crept by like molasses. I can't tell you how much you've been missed. In case you're wondering, yes, I still hang around with Mike. He's not the little pervert he once was. In fact, he's quite a decent guy. One of the most reliable friends I've had since you. I am glad I finally got to meet your family. They were really incredible people. I particularly liked your older brother. He was a decent guy. I'm sorry to say we haven't been in touch in years, though, and I find myself wondering how they all are doing.

Speaking of family, I've got one of my own now! Can you believe that shit? Yep, I've got a little girl and a little boy. I was married, but not anymore. I had the little girl when I was married, and she's five now. Her name is Mackenzie. We named her after the alpha female wolf at the International Wolf Center in Ely, Minnesota. I know what you're thinking. Minnesota? But it was a really cool place to live, for real. I've always been a big fan of wolves, too, and the name just stuck. I have a tattoo of a wolf on my left arm to symbolize her. I wish so much you could have met her. She's such a smart, outgoing girl.

I also have a little boy. He's only a couple of months old, but he's already full of personality. I had him with my girlfriend. I never planned on having any kids without being married. But hey, I also never planned on being divorced in my thirties. I know, it sucks. But sometimes these things just happen. The reason for my divorce? Mostly me. I'm just a guy who's got lots of emotional issues, from depression to anxiety to insecurity, and those issues unfortunately caused quite a strain on the marriage. At least we're being civil to one another.

Back to the boy. The little guy's name is Mingus. We named him after a famous jazz bassist, Charles Mingus. I wonder how many kids you would've had if you were still here? It would've been so cool for our families to get together on weekends for barbecues and football.

I haven't seen or heard from most of the guys in years. I wish I knew what Mack was up to, but we lost touch while I was still in college. I don't even live in New York anymore. Man, I've been all over the place. And I mean that literally. I'm a writer, so traveling around is just a part of my job. I've been all over the world. You should see my passport! My favorite place? Paris.

Henry, I can't tell you enough times how sorry I am. One of the thoughts that continues to haunt me is whether or not you realized that what I did was an accident. I really hope you did. I hope you knew there was no way I would hurt you on purpose. I wish there was something I could do to right the wrongs of what I did. It was so fucking stupid, I still can't believe I didn't know better.

I really do want to get this thing sorted out between us. I've always been willing to do whatever it takes to do right by you. Unfortunately, trying to figure out the best way to do so had me running in circles. Eventually I burned myself out, and I'm just now pulling myself out of the hole I'd fallen into. I don't want to ever fall into that hole again. I hope you understand. And I hope one day my being sorry will be enough.

• • •

Henry is dead, and I killed him. I don't know if I ever will truly be able to be absolved of that sin. I'm not certain true redemption can ever come for someone who has done the things I have. What I do know is that living my own life is now hard enough that I can no longer try to live for two people, one of whom I can never bring back. I think Henry was a better person than me. But I no longer think I'm the worst person in the world.

There are still many more things I know I need to do. One day, I need to work up the courage to find and speak to Henry's family again. I need to visit Henry's grave, which I was unable to do after the wake. I need to find some of those mutual friends who have been lost in the ether for so long. It's a checklist, and I realize I might not be able to do everything on my list. Indeed, it's taken me nearly sixteen years just to come to terms with the incident itself (item number one on my list), and with my family's medical history, I don't think I'll be around to see one hundred—either years or item number on my checklist.

Until then, I still have a life to live. I have others for whom I'm now responsible. Not just my daughter Mackenzie, but a little son, Mingus. I'm hoping his life won't mirror the one Charles Mingus recounts in *Beneath the Underdog*. Brooding over myself will only make their lives more difficult. At least that's one thing that I can tell myself to make it a bit easier to sleep at night. In the end, what is absolution anyway? No person can declare absolution if our heart does not believe it. No amount of good deeds, no amount of effort, will ever absolve me of Henry's death. Because he should not have died. That should have never happened. He should be here with me right now. We should be playing with each other's kids. We should be reminiscing about Brooklyn.

Instead, Brooklyn is a distant memory now. A place I can't return to—even if I moved back to New York again. Brooklyn died with Henry; I can only go back to it in my dreams. I sometimes wonder if this internal dialogue goes on in the minds of everyone who commits a heinous act. If the thousands of inmates on Riker's Island spend their quiet evenings playing out all of their mistakes in their heads, wondering how they came to be where they are. Wondering what the families of their victim(s) are doing. How they're getting by. How their own family is handling the shame of their actions. I'm not a convict in the eyes of the law, and I've never seen the inside of a prison. Still, in many ways, I believe those inmates alone in their cells are the people whose routine thoughts most closely mirror mine. You've got a lot of time to think when you're sitting in a cell, whether the walls of it are lined with concrete or skull.

I awaken to the whirring of helicopter blades overhead. Being in Los Angeles is peculiar. I hadn't realized how accustomed I was to the night sounds of car alarms and conversation until they were replaced with the whirring blades of passing helicopters. Sometimes they were news helicopters, tracking traffic on the nearby 10 freeway or some random police chase. Usually, they were police copters, shining a light into a neighborhood alley to help the cops on the ground flush out some petty criminal.

If you'd have told me a decade ago I'd be living in L.A. today,

I would have laughed in your face. Los Angeles is a city I'd hated long before I ever set foot in it. Maybe it's because L.A. symbolizes everything that isn't New York. I'd heard all of the horror stories. The smog is so bad you can get asthma during a weekend visit. The Bloods and Crips will accost anyone wearing any article of clothing that's one of their gang colors, red or blue. It takes an hour to get anywhere, and you need a car to do anything. L.A. sounded like hell on Earth, and my first trip did little to discount any of those stereotypes. I spent almost my entire time in the backseat of a friend's car, and I didn't see a single thing that would have sparked an interest in returning.

But I did return anyway. On many occasions. L.A. was a big enough city that there was always some story or project that would force me to come out. And then a funny thing happened between the first and the twentieth trip to the City of Angels; I actually came to like the place. It was a peculiar coincidence that as New York became more and more foreign to me, Los Angeles became more and more comfortable. It was as though the two cities underwent a gradual personality transplant. New York became a glistening tourist destination, and the population transformed from a solid working class (with a smattering of rarely seen aristocracy) to a place where even people barely skirting the poverty line outwardly appeared wealthy. Women wearing two-hundred-dollar designer shoes would die of starvation if there weren't free buffets at the parties they were attending.

Meanwhile, L.A. became the city of broken dreams and broken promises. It was more maligned than any big city in the country. When people said Los Angeles, the immediate images were crime, traffic, pollution, and corruption. Racial tension had sparked the L.A. riots in the nineties, and the area had never recovered. San Francisco and San Diego had become the desirable, livable cities of California. L.A. was the shit hole. In fact, the descriptions of Los Angeles began to sound eerily like the descriptions of New York City that I'd heard growing up.

I always thought the place lacked New York's character, but it never seemed *that* bad. It was large and unruly, to be sure, but hardly the sprawling suburban nightmare that people described. If you wanted a suburban nightmare, you could head to Atlanta or Chicago. Los Angeles bore little resemblance to those cities. It did, however, bear a tremendous resemblance to the enormous, sprawling cities of South America. Places like Buenos Aires, which were anything but suburban, but had developed in a haphazard fashion, overwhelming the landscape from which the city originally sprouted.

Los Angeles was a real city, where one could have the kind of anonymity that was impossible any place outside of New York. The bright façade of stardom was quickly washed away after the tenth or so encounter with your favorite celebrity in the aisles of a local Ralph's supermarket, their skin pock-marked as they argued with a cashier over usage of certain coupons. I couldn't help but marvel at how bad so many of the female celebrities looked in person when they were buying their groceries or walking the aisles of a local Blockbuster video. In contrast, the male celebrities almost always looked even better than they did on-screen. Perfect skin, perfect teeth, perfect hair. It was like some twisted gender reversal happened when the cameras stopped rolling.

Los Angeles was a place where people could still afford to

live. It was a place where there were still starving artists. A place where the reality was nowhere near as good or as bad as the stories. It was a place that began to feel like home. I found myself in Los Angeles because of the last attempt Nicole and I made to reconcile. Our previous destinations held too many bad memories, and we figured we would give our marriage one more shot in a new locale where neither of us had roots. Los Angeles beat out San Francisco by a slim margin thanks to its cheaper rents and better weather. Plus, we figured, if things didn't work out, it was one of the only cities left in the country that was big enough for both of us.

Things in fact did not work out, and we nearly tore each other's heads off on our ride to Los Angeles. We lived under the same roof for just a month before we went our separate ways one final time. It was strange being alone in such a huge new place, and I began to kill time by exploring. I'd drive my car from one end of the city to the other, finding small nooks at which to hang out. I took up my favorite pastime of whiling away hours in bookstores—of which there were a surprisingly large number. There were always readings or other events that were interesting and free. My daughter also enjoys visiting bookstores, so on the days when I have her with me, we usually spend at least an hour in a bookstore, where she always suckers me into buying her a new book. I don't mind. In fact, I like the fact that she's so enthusiastic about reading. I was also an enthusiastic reader as a young child, and I don't think there's such a thing as too much reading. Maybe when she's older I'll pass on some deeper material to her.

On this particular day I'm walking through a mall on my way to a book reading. My cell phone rings, and the caller ID says that it's Mom. That's unusual, since Mom doesn't call me very much anymore, so I take a detour and answer my telephone.

"Hi, Kemp, it's Mom."

I don't like the tone of her voice. I'm really not in the mood for any bad news these days. It's why I've stopped answering my cell phone in general. I've become weary of feeling like all those with bad tidings have got a tracking device on me thanks to my cell phone.

"I read your story."

I'm shocked. I'd written a recount of the Shooting for *Esquire* magazine that was published in December 2002. I never expected Mom to read it. She knew I'd written it, but hadn't spoken to me about it since that telephone call after the family gathering back in Brooklyn. And now it was September 2003, and I was getting this call?

"Your sister brought the story over and let me read it."

Now I was confused. Why would one of my sisters do that? I'd soon find out my estranged wife had told one of my sisters I was working on a book that was going to mention all of them, and reminded them that the article was already published. My sister decided to go to a local library and procure a copy of the article herself.

"I thought I was doing you a favor by not talking about this. I didn't know that you were still so upset by this. That it was so much on your mind. You know, I'll talk to you about it whenever you want. You know that I love you."

She pauses to wait for my response, but one won't be coming. I've spent my entire life shouldering the burden of Henry's death, trying to find a release. When I finally found something that could be considered a pseudoresolution, it just dragged me down to a depth from which I'd only recently managed to surface. It's been such a big part of me for so long, I don't even remember who I was before Henry died, and I no longer wanted to anymore. Whoever I was before the Shooting died right along with Henry on my bedroom floor.

Once again, I can only say all of these things in my own head. I just wait in silence on the other end. I wait for Mom to say good-bye and let me hang up. This time I'm the one waiting to be released.

EPILOGUE

This book was written in transit, both literally and metaphorically. I wrote while I sat on airplanes, rode in cabs, and sat alone in hotels. They seemed to be the only times I could get comfortable enough to sit down and rehash the old thoughts and feelings. By the time I neared the end of this project, I was able to sit at my desk at home and write for hours at a time without the chills running down my spine. That's a small victory, and I hope I have many more like it over the years.

As I wrote this book, my life also went through a very dynamic transition. I continue to strive for perfection in everything that I do, but now I realize that I am far from, and never will be, perfect. Still, I can make a significant mark on the world as a writer, a parent, a black man, and a human being. I can do these things despite the Shooting.

The Shooting is not my life. It is not all that I am. I am a writer who's traveled the world. I'm a father with two children. I'm a failed husband and a hopeful son. I'm a good friend to some, a decent associate to others. *The Shooting is not my life.* It was a terrible chapter of it. It's a part of me, and it always will be, but it does not define who I am. I could talk to you for hours about politics, the environment, and music. I could talk to you forever about Brooklyn, the city that raised me, and the greatest place on Earth. I have ideas and stories, enough to fill a library. I can even talk to you about Henry and the great person he was. I just hope I've said all I need to say about the Shooting.

My daughter is about to turn six, and is both lovely and precocious. Her health problems have vanished, and it's no longer necessary to treat her like a piece of fine china. She certainly doesn't see herself that way, as her weekly bumps, bruises, and cuts will attest. My son is an infant, and I hold so much hope for him and what I know he is capable of. I'm comfortable being left alone with him. I know things can happen, bad things, but all I can do is face them head-on. Besides, he's entirely too cute for me not to enjoy.

I hope both of my kids grow up to be good people. The types of people who make everyone around them so happy, so fulfilled, that their absence is a tragedy. That's the type of person Henry was. It's the type of person I'd hoped to become in his absence. It's the type of person I may still one day become, if I can ever get my life completely back on track. I'm certainly on my way.

Am I better? It depends on how one defines "better." I'm more comfortable in my own skin. I can walk forward without looking back. I have hope once again. I also have a new sense of relief about getting my story out there, as insignificant as it may be. If I am to be judged, I prefer to be judged by my own words, so if even one person reads it, then this fifteen-years-in-the-making story has already served its purpose.